NELSON – METCALFE, M.
book should be   ed to any branch   the
    shire Coun   or before   wn

IMAGES OF ENGLAND

NELSON

D0274500

IMAGES OF ENGLAND

NELSON

MARILYN METCALFE

TEMPUS

0877765735

Frontispiece: Mr Sharp and his daughter Mrs Gee standing at the door of their shop at No. 51 Manchester Road in around 1920. John Watson, a stationer, newsagent and advertising agent at No. 8 Manchester Road, printed *The Colne and Nelson Times* newspaper and also the *Colne and Nelson Express* for many years.

First published 2005

Tempus Publishing Limited
The Mill, Brimscombe Port,
Stroud, Gloucestershire, GL5 2QG
www.tempus-publishing.com

© Marilyn Metcalfe, 2005

The right of Marilyn Metcalfe to be identified as the Author
of this work has been asserted in accordance with the
Copyrights, Designs and Patents Act 1988.

All rights reserved. No part of this book may be reprinted
or reproduced or utilised in any form or by any electronic,
mechanical or other means, now known or hereafter invented,
including photocopying and recording, or in any information
storage or retrieval system, without the permission in writing
from the Publishers.

British Library Cataloguing in Publication Data.
A catalogue record for this book is available from the British Library.

ISBN 0 7524 3630 9

Typesetting and origination by Tempus Publishing Limited.
Printed in Great Britain.

Contents

Acknowledgements

My special thanks go to the staff at the Nelson Library, in particular Mrs C. Carradice, the reference librarian, who has kindly loaned me numerous photographs for publication in this book. Also I am grateful to Mr J. Bentley, who let me borrow his 'Nelson' albums containing old postcards, several of which have been used in the following chapters. I thank my friend Fran Wilkinson for allowing me to draw on her computing expertise.

An article appeared in the *Nelson Leader* newspaper, for which I thank Mr P. Dewhirst, asking for photographs and ephemera that could be included in this book. A second article sought identification of three photographs featured. I thank the many people who responded to these articles. They include Mrs D. Sheppy, Mrs S. Oldfield, Mrs C. Boothman, Mr M. Head, Mrs J. Sedman, Mr J. Heaton and Mr S. Berry. I also thank Mrs A. Sutton, Mrs L.A. Dole, Mrs P. Hudson, Mr S. Farnell, Mr W. Proctor, Mr D. Hanson, Mr S. Barnes, Mr G. Eyre, Mr G. Yates and others who provided interesting material following my phone calls. Many of the photographs and materials loaned from them appear in this book.

Finally I wish to express my gratitude to Mrs S. Byrne, former reference librarian, for allowing me to use some of the material she has researched.

Introduction

Marsden, of which Nelson forms a large part, has a history dating back to the time of William the Conqueror. However, Nelson as a town dates back only 140 years and as a result had less slum property than many large manufacturing towns in Lancashire. The majority of its mills and workshops were also constructed after 1850, an exception being a small mill at Edge End built by the Ecroyd family in 1740.

Two hundred years ago the view from Marsden Heights in Little Marsden would have been of mainly agricultural land, with a few hamlets and small villages dotted here and there. There were two coal mines, one close to the Chapel Inn and one near to the Heights. The Kippax family of Scholefield was influential in the area. The Conformists had Little Marsden Chapel, later called St Paul's. A meeting house for the Religious Society of Friends (or Quakers) was established close by at Edge End as early as 1660. The Congregationalists, possibly as many as 400, worshipped at Providence Church, a little above Edge End, from around 1839. Churches and Sunday schools often acted as social centres. There were several public houses and beer shops but no theatres, billiard rooms or dance halls.

In Great Marsden, the Walton family was associated with Marsden Hall for centuries. The Hartley family owned Bradley Hall, and other prominent families included the Every-Clayton's of Carr Hall and the Sagar's of Southfield.

Many of the local people were farmers or farm labourers who grew oats and wheat on enclosed land. In addition many were engaged in the wool and cotton trades. Handloom weaving was a skilful operation and at the beginning of the nineteenth century good weavers were able to earn up to £1 per week. However, machinery began to replace handwork and much distress was suffered after 1825. Some weavers were earning as little as six shillings, less than one third of the wages they had earned at the beginning of the century! Although others in the area were employed as builders, wheelwrights and in other trades, the destitution of the weavers affected them adversely.

Several factors contributed to the advancement of Nelson in Marsden. There were better roads between the counties of Lancashire and Yorkshire and the construction of the Leeds to Burnley section of the Leeds & Liverpool Canal opened in 1796. Probably the most important factor was the opening of the East Lancashire Railway in 1849. The town's new railway station was given the name Nelson and the area's names of Great and Little Marsden were mostly replaced by that of Nelson, although its acreage was about three quarters that of the whole of Marsden.

In 1850 B. and J. Smith, from Colne, erected Walverden Mill in Leeds Road. At about the same time John Walton built the earliest part of Holme Mill for his two sons, James and Joshua. The top room was used for spinning cotton and the bottom one for weaving. Richard and Haworth Sagar erected Throstle Nest Mills in the Bradley area. The builders of Victoria Mills in Leeds Road, Messrs Whitehead and Holland, were not manufacturers; they provided space and power for others. Therefore men with only enough capital to purchase machinery could begin production straight away. This system was later adopted on a wide scale.

The district around the Centre began to expand dramatically and the Select Vestry's twenty members had little power to regulate the building of cottages, make provision for sanitary arrangements or provide an adequate supply of water for domestic uses. Water for drinking and washing was taken from the river or drawn from wells and every house possessed a large tub for rainwater collection. There was no public gas supply and the mills had to make and store their own. It became apparent to the leading men in the town that a better form of local government was vitally important if further progress was to be made. A quarry owner, Mr Benjamin Chaffer, called the ratepayers to a meeting in Salem Chapel on August 24 1864 and the adoption of the Local Government Act 1858 was considered. A poll was demanded and granted and voting papers were delivered on October 7.

On 15 October 1864, the *Advertiser* reported that 'On Monday night October 10th there was great excitement in consequence of a report that some persons had entered the district for the purpose of getting hold of the voting papers, it was conjectured, in order to make away with them.' The suspected persons were chased a considerable distance and did not return as they were put in fear of their lives! On 12 October the poll declared in favour of adoption. A Local Board was formed and twelve members were elected. Mr Tunstill of Reedyford was the first chairman. Immediately they set about forming committees and appointing the necessary officials. However it was not until 1872 that the first accountant for the town was selected. John Elliott was appointed as bookkeeper and collector on 1 June with a renumerative of £70 a year. He had worked as a shop man for the Co-operative Society when aged twelve. The first important work was to secure an Act of Parliament to get gas and water supplies to the people of Nelson, and the Act received royal assent in June 1866. The Board was authorised to take water from the Catlow Brook and also to purchase the Leeds Road Gasworks from the Nelson Gas Company. On 23 November 1889 a ratepayers' petition was sent to Queen Victoria requesting a Charter of Incorporation.

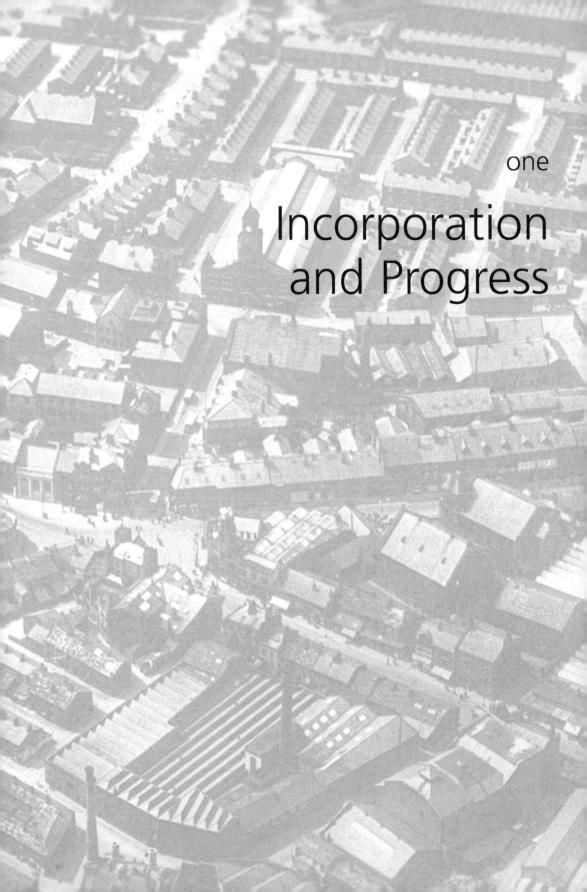

one

Incorporation
and Progress

A triumphal arch was erected on Scotland Road to celebrate Nelson's incorporation on 21 July 1890. The arch was 6ft through with a centre span of 18ft. It was constructed from evergreens, and the royal arms and flags surmounted the structure. Messrs W.E. Coar (grocer), J. Fielding (furniture dealer), Manley and Hartley (ironmongers) and other tradesmen met the costs. A banner with the words 'God bless our Queen' was outside Mr Coar's shop.

Samuel Gott, a native of Cowling, came to the Marsden area with his family before Nelson had emerged. Mr Gott was a tailor, first working for Mr McMillan. His eldest child Sarah helped him when he had his own shop at 1-3 Railway Street. He bought the first sewing machine that came to Nelson, for £30, and later he was a draper at 58 Manchester Road. Mr Gott was involved in the establishment of the Local Board in 1864 and was elected to that body; he was the chairman of several important committees and also taught evening classes. In 1890 he became Nelson's first mayor and held office for twelve months. Following the death of his wife, Mr Gott moved with his daughters to Blackpool and died on 1 January 1905, aged eighty-one.

These are some of Nelson's aldermen and councillors in 1890/91. From left to right, standing:
Councillor John Haytock (cotton manufacturer), Councillor William Ward (secretary of Nelson Textile
Trade Federation), Mr S Boodman, Councillor Joseph Pickles Sunderland (cotton manufacturer), -
?- , -?- , -?- . Sitting: Councillor Smith Hudson, Councillor Richard Smith (boot and shoemaker),
Dr Jackson, Alderman John Wilkinson (cotton manufacturer), Mr R.M. Prescott, Alderman William
Landless, Councillor John Sagar, Councillor William Reed (cotton manufacturer). Front: Councillor
Lawrence Tattersall (bookseller and stationer), Councillor William Dyson (cotton manufacturer). Richard
Melling Prescott was born on 10 February 1860. When only twenty-one years of age he was appointed
secretary to the Association of Local Board Clerks of England and Wales. He was interested in police
administration and was editor of the queries department of the official newspaper, the *Police Chronicle*.
Mr Prescott continued with this work after his appointment as Nelson Town Clerk on 3 October 1888.
It was he who influenced the Local Board to make application for the town to become a borough. The
cost of Nelson's charter, granted by Queen Victoria, was only £69! Mr Prescott resigned as town clerk at
the end of March 1901.

The town hall was built in 1881. Following an enquiry at the Council chambers in January 1892 regarding a loan of £32,000 for extensions and improvements, a town clerk's office and a police station were added in 1893 and a technical school was erected in 1895. King George V and Queen Mary's Silver Jubilee was on 5 May 1935 and the *Nelson Leader* newspaper carried the headline 'Socialist Councillors Outwitted by Loyal Citizens'. During the night of 6 May a few locals painted part of an outside wall of Nelson's town hall red, white and blue!

Left: This centenary medallion was a popular purchase in 1990. In July 1890 the tender of Alfred Richardson, watch and clock maker of 38 Manchester Road was accepted for 4,000 inscribed medals, to be given to Nelson's scholars to celebrate the incorporation. The borough received its grant of armorial bearings on 22 October 1890. Nelson's motto is 'By Industry and Integrity'.

Opposite below: Robert Hartley and Richard Elliott first worked the Catlow Quarries in the 1830s and Richard's sons Francis, John and Henry were also quarrymen there. One winter in the 1840s Henry was 'frozen out' at the quarry. By good fortune his son Thomas, when on his way to the post office near Lomeshaye Lane top, discovered two one-shilling pieces embedded in the frozen ground. The family's diet at the time was mainly porridge, but on that day they sat down to a royal feast of bread! The majority of houses in Nelson were built from Catlow stone. This picture shows quarrymen in around 1930.

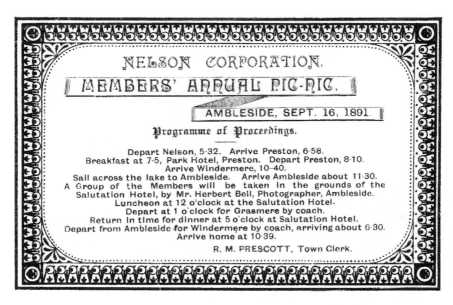

NELSON CORPORATION.

MEMBERS' ANNUAL PIC-NIC.

AMBLESIDE, SEPT. 16, 1891.

Programme of Proceedings.

Depart Nelson, 5·32.   Arrive Preston, 6·58.
Breakfast at 7·5, Park Hotel, Preston.   Depart Preston, 8·10.
Arrive Windermere, 10–40.
Sail across the lake to Ambleside.   Arrive Ambleside about 11·30.
A Group of the Members will be taken in the grounds of the
Salutation Hotel, by Mr. Herbert Bell, Photographer, Ambleside.
Luncheon at 12 o'clock at the Salutation Hotel.
Depart at 1 o'clock for Grasmere by coach.
Return in time for dinner at 5 o'clock at Salutation Hotel.
Depart from Ambleside for Windermere by coach, arriving about 6·30.
Arrive home at 10·39.

R. M. PRESCOTT, Town Clerk.

Above: The times listed for this excursion to the Lake District, organised for Corporation employees in 1891 by Nelson's town clerk, appear to be precise in every detail. The early starting time of 5.32 a.m. is worthy of note

The Nelson Fire Brigade was formed 8 March 1873 and eight firemen were appointed. The horses that pulled the engine were also used by the Cleansing Department, and when the town hall bells sounded they were unyoked and taken to the fire station as quickly as possible. This shows the 'bugle boy' and firemen in around 1891 with the *Lord Nelson* steam engine, which was paraded through the town on Charter Day. In 1902 the *Marsden* engine was purchased. The *Lord Nelson* became redundant in February 1914 when a motor engine was acquired.

Tradesmen had been working long hours in July 1890 to complete the new fire station off Carr Road in time for Charter Day and the reception of the *Lord Nelson*. In September 1891 the alarm bells were transferred from the town hall to the fire station. This photograph was taken in around 1936. The firemen are pictured with, from left to right, three ambulances, a Rolls Royce, the *Alderman Boothman* (purchased in 1936) and the *Braidwood* (purchased in May 1932).

These officers certainly look a stern bunch on this photograph from around 1894, taken in front of the police station on Cross Street. The gentleman standing in the doorway wearing a top hat is Nelson's town clerk, Mr Prescott. In the late 1830s the Marsden Vestry Committee lost the right to appoint part-time police constables, paid £4 a year, when the Lancashire Constabulary was formed, consisting of full-time, fully trained men. Henry Elliott, relieving officer of Lee Farm Swinden, was the last Marsden police constable.

These are St John Ambulance workers with their new ambulance wagon in around 1892. One Saturday morning in November 1891 nearly £39 was collected in local mills and workshops towards the purchase of a wagon costing £90. It was expected that the total amount needed would come from public subscriptions. Livery stables owner James Clegg Hartley provided a horse and driver free and Robert Thornton of Manchester Road also accompanied every case to hospital.

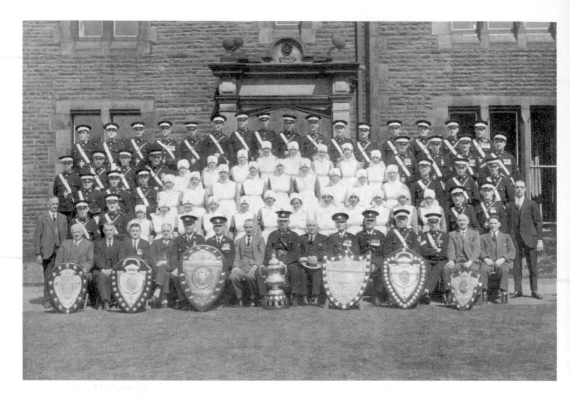

Above: The Nelson Ambulance Corps had an outstanding success in 1928. The 'competition squad' went to London to compete in a national competition. The squad was placed first and won the Dewar Shield. On the following day they proceeded to Blackpool, where they were again placed first in a competition and won the Argenta Cup.

Left: Richard Townsley was born in Little Marsden in 1862, a son of 'bill poster' and choirmaster Richard Townsley. Young Richard became a cotton weaver at nine years of age. He was appointed Town Crier for Little Marsden in 1878 and for the borough in 1901. A valued member of the Nelson Salvation Army, Mr Townsley later moved to Blackpool. On 22 January 1933 at the Blackpool Salvation Army Citadel, he suddenly collapsed, still clutching his Bible, and was pronounced dead shortly afterwards.

This picture shows the post office, erected in 1893 at the end of Tickle Street. Mr Walter Woodhouse was the first postmaster there. Nelson's first post office was established on 2 September 1839 in a cottage on Leeds Road and James Holt was postmaster and shoemaker. His son-in-law was in charge when the post office was on Manchester Road in the 1850s. Between 1865 and 1893 it operated from the printers and stationers at 18-20 Railway Street, where James Banks Whitham was postmaster. He also produced much of the literature for Charter Day.

Public Library, Nelson

David Rushton became the librarian when the free library was opened on 27 April 1890, in an upper room in the market hall. In 1895 a joint library and technical school was opened. However, larger premises were needed and Sir Andrew Carnegie kindly gave a grant of £7,000 towards the cost. Arthur Henderson MP officially opened this new library in Carr Road on 29 February 1908.

The Nelson Local Board obtained an order to supply electricity in 1883 and a plant was installed at the Leeds Road Gasworks. The generator's 100kW capacity assisted the Gas Department in the development of lighting. Owing to increased demands the new electricity works on Charles Street (adjoining the Refuse Destructor) were opened on 12 March 1902. This photograph is from around 1903.

Opposte above: The Tunstill family's former home at Reedyford became the memorial hospital. By May 1920 organiser Councillor W. Riley had received offers of subscriptions from 4,000 people, in addition to donations. Reedyford was by this time fully staffed, and twenty-four inpatients and around sixty-five disabled soldiers were receiving treatment. The house surgeon Dr Watson had already carried out a number of operations.

Opposite below: William Brown (1838-1876) of Messrs Brown & Astley, brewers, built Fern Lea on part of Netherfield Farm. Following his partner's death William Astley (1840-1896) bought the house for £655. William Astley's widow Ann, the mother of eight children, donated the house to the town in 1911 as a memorial to King Edward. It became the Nelson and District Queen's Nurses Home and in early May 1919 was opened as a maternity home for ten patients, run by the Nelson and District Nursing Association. The home closed in 1968.

WALVERDEN RESERVIOR - NELSON

Above: Walverden Reservoir in around 1900. By the 1880s the Local Board had waterworks equal to the demands of a population of 100,000, the expenditure for building being around £64,000. These valuable undertakings were at Walverden, Coldwell and Pendle, all acquired after 1870. In June 1891 William Jones, previously employed on the Manchester Ship Canal, became the clerk of works for the new reservoir at Black Moss. It would be capable of holding 40 million gallons.

Left: Andrew Smith (later Sir Andrew Smith) was elected to the Town Council on 22 November 1911 and was the first chairman of the Nelson Housing Committee. He was elected mayor in 1927. His unstinting work for the town was honoured when a new home for the elderly was given his name. The £41,000 hostel on Marsden Hall Road, opened in 1958, provided comfortable accommodation for fifty aged persons. How very different from the days when Mr Smith sat on the Board of Guardians battling for downtrodden people fated to end their days in the workhouse.

Councillor Elihu Wilkinson, chairman of the Nelson Education Committee, formally opened the new council schools on Bradshaw Street in April 1908. The total cost of building was £12,000. There were three schools, each with a large hall providing accommodation for 1,160 infant, junior and senior children in twenty-two classrooms. After the opening a banquet was served to Mr Wilkinson's guests at the town hall. Most appropriately the final course was 'Education Pudding'! Mr J. Gill was the first headmaster.

Marsden Park was opened to the public on 20 June 1912. In June 1920 plans were being prepared for the building of a bandstand and in June 1924 tennis courts were opened. John Thornber and Mr Kippax designed the sundial in the park. When it was first erected it indicated the time in twelve different parts of the world.

WALVERDEN PARK - NELSON (2)

Victoria Park Nelson. 1163.

These builders, employed by the Stanworth Bros, are outside a terrace house in Nelson in around 1914. Private individuals financed the building of many houses up to this time. William Stanworth, a slate merchant, was probably the founder of the company. The partnership between William Hartley Dyson and John Stanworth, builders, was dissolved on 28 February 1910, and a new business was formed and run by the Stanworth family.

An entry in the Colne Parish Church Records, made nearly 100 years before this photograph was taken, reads, 'Levi Stanworth – plaisterer'.

Opposite above: Land measuring 8 ½ acres and costing £900 was purchased from Mr H.M. Walton in 1897. This made a total of just over 20 acres for a park at Walverden. The park was opened on 30 May 1900. On Wednesday 13 July 1910 a large number of interested spectators gathered at the park gates to see a party of elderly men, including Thomas Elliott and Duckworth Tattersall, both aged seventy-six, board a wagonette driven by John Varley. This group of men, whose average age was seventy-one, had met regularly in the park shelter to discuss any topic of interest. Before their departure to Gisburn, where tea would be served, the Park Authorities kindly presented each man with a buttonhole. This card was postmarked at 7.30 p.m. on 4 July 1912.

Opposite below: In February 1896 the Messrs Dickson submitted a plan to the Parks Committee. Their scheme suggested that the four divisions of the park, caused by the river and road, be brought into one by means of grotto archways under the road and artistic bridges. Victoria Park was first opened to the public on 27 April 1896. A bowling green costing £450 was opened on 25 May 1903.

The gasworks in Leeds Road, Nelson was acquired in 1886 at a cost of £8,887 10s. An application was made in December 1909 by Nelson Town Council for authorisation to borrow £13,000 for new gas mains and meters, to meet the needs of a growing population. This picture is of Nelson's No. 1 gas workers gang in the 1920s. Shortly afterwards, gas production in Nelson was abandoned and moved to Brierfield.

This is an aerial view of Nelson taken in around 1925 showing the main streets radiating from the Centre, where the clock tower can be seen. The market hall on Market Street is clearly visible left of centre. The weaving mills in the foreground are on Leeds Road.

two

Saving and Spending

This photograph shows a section of the Marsden Building Society Banking Hall. The preliminary meeting of the founders took place at the home of Mr Thomas Holland of Woodlands. The minute book of the society reports as follows: 'On Wednesday evening, 29th February, 1860, a number of persons were met at the house of Mr Thomas Holland. The conversation turned upon the scarcity of cottages in the neighbourhood and the pressing demand for suitable dwellings for its rapidly increasing population.' A committee was formed and architect Mr Smith Whitehead was elected as chairman, with Mr Waddington as secretary. The rules were drawn up and submitted to a meeting of shareholders held at the Oddfellows Club on April 14. The society came into existence on 8 May 1860 under the title of 'Great and Little Marsden Permanent Benefit Building Society'.

Mr Briarley of Bury bought the old Nelson Arcade, comprising twenty-three shops and warehouses, in June 1907 for £10,300, so that the Union Bank could build a branch. At the beginning of May 1910 the Union Bank agreed to rebuild their premises eight yards further back, as the Centre was to be widened. At the end of October 1910 a public clock was erected over the bank in memory of Mr W.C. Murgatroyd, secretary of the Education Committee.

TO BE SOLD

BY AUCTION, BY

MR. J. BROWN,

At the House and Premises of
Mr. J. Dixon, Lower Bradley, Little Marsden,
On Thursday, Sept. 22nd, 1864,
THE FOLLOWING FARMING

STOCK

10 HEAD OF HORNED CATTLE, & 4 SUMMER CALVES,
Viz: 2 Cows to calve in October, 1 Cow lately calven, 1
Cow to calve in February, 2 Bulled Cows, very fresh in
Milk, 2 Spring calving Heifers, 2 Stirks; 1 Brood Mare,
12 years old, 14½ hands high; 1 Colt rising 3 years, fit for
Saddle or Harness; 2 Young Sows, of a first rate breed;
Two store Pigs, 1 Cart with 4½ Inch Wheels, 1 do with
narrow Wheels, Plough & Harrows, 2 Sets of Cart Gears,
1 Hackney Saddle, and 2 Bridles, 1 Churn, 3 good Lead
Milk Bowls, Butter Bowl, Milking Tins & Sile, 2 Copper
Kettles, 1 Brass Pan, 1 Oak Chest, 1 Clock, 1 corner Cup-
board, Four Chairs, And a variety of other Articles too
numerous to mention. Also 190 yards of

WELL-GOT HAY,

to be Sold in Lots, to be consumed on the Premises. The
Fog and Winter Herbage of the whole Farm, until the
26th of April, 1865. Sale to commence at 12 o'clock
at noon, when the time of payment will be fixed.
J. HARTLEY, PRINTER AND BOOKSELLER, COLNE.

An auction of stock held at Lower Bradley Farm ('a roomy farmhouse, not very lofty, but its external appearance was its great beauty'). The farmhouse itself must have been sold shortly afterwards, as Thomas and Sarah Rycroft were living there with their five children by 1871. Later it was known as Pollard's Tenement. The building was eventually pulled down for the gasworks extension.

Above: On one side of Bradley Row were five houses with one-room cellar dwellings. On the opposite side was a row of old cottages known as Bog Row. James Duerden owned an old country store at the top end from around 1840. Bunches of candles, hams, swilling and black lead brushes hung from the low ceiling. On 27 October 1860 the Revd John Henderson married Joseph Snowden and Ellen Duerden, who had been born at the shop in 1843. The bridesmaids wore Paisley shawls and a fiddler supplied the music! Mr Snowden owned the store after his father-in-law retired in around 1875.

This is Clark's hardware business at 52-56 Leeds Road in the 1940s. Their premises were formerly cottages and the Kay family had lived in one of them in the 1880s (the bedroom windows are clearly visible). The business was here for fifty years, until a move in 1972 to 1-5 Pendle Street. In 1981 a total refurbishment was carried out at the present premises on Every Street (built as a fish market in 1891), and the store was reopened as G.A. Clark (Hardware) Ltd In September 1982. The company's diamond jubilee was celebrated in October 1982.

Opposite below: Thornton Clark first worked as a saddler in Barrowford in 1849. By 1855 he had moved to Little Marsden and in 1871 he was living at 1 Leeds Road with his family. The business remained at these premises, becoming Thornton Clark & Sons. By 1883 Mr William Clark (the older son) was head of the firm, now at 4 Leeds Road. He died aged forty-three in October 1896, leaving a widow and six children. This photograph is of a shop display at 4 Leeds Road for the centenary in 1949 of the founding of the firm. The premises were demolished in October 1967.

Henry Varley from Bacup convinced James Bateson of Nelson of the benefits to be gained from a Co-operative store and a first meeting of the Nelson Co-operative Society was held in the weft-room at Lomeshaye Mill in early 1860. A group of 'Old Pioneers' is pictured here on the recreation ground for the society's Golden Jubilee in 1910. From left to right: William Hargreaves, Thomas Willock, Thomas Elliott, Peter Aldersley, Moses Brown, the Revd Elliott, James Widmore, Joseph Edmondson, William Edmondson, Joseph Bradshaw, John Whittaker.

Opposite above: The clothing departments from the Co-operative premises at the corner of Albert Road and Manchester Road were transferred to the central premises on Leeds Road in 1895. The styles of the ladies garments date this photograph to the time of the First World War. The new frontage was certainly added after 1910.

Opposite below: The Co-operative Society's No. 7 Branch on Larch Street opened in March 1890. Manager Joseph Catlow (far right) and four assistants are seen here standing outside the store at the turn of the twentieth century. Although the shop may appear to be over-staffed, this was a time when every customer received personal service. There was a butchery department next door.

This is the No. 20 Branch Co-operative Store in Brunswick Street, opened in March 1908. A lady passing the Brunswick Street Store at 11.55 p.m. on 24 December 1913 saw two figures moving inside carrying lighted tapers. These men were arrested and charged with stealing four keys, some foreign coins, ¾lb of cheese, cake, ginger ale, an ounce of tobacco, chocolate and pomfret cakes with a total value of 4s 1ld. One pleaded guilty, the other not guilty!

Walter Lambert, born at Colne in 1860, worked in a mill after he left school. By the 1880s he had a successful business at 9 Scotland Road, Nelson, making cricket bats and mending bats for the Nelson Cricket Club. Mr Lambert took over a joinery business on Cross Street in around 1889, adding stables and several lock-up shops. He purchased the large horizontal sawing machine from the Albert Hall (Nelson) joinery works in June 1891, shortly before this photograph was taken.

CHINA & JAPAN!

ABM. ALTHAM

Has made a Special Purchase of Vases, Spill Pots, Hand Screens, Trays, Fans, Pomatum Pots, Bamboo Bread  and Japan. These Goods will be offered on **THURSDAY NEXT**, and following days, at such Low Prices as will surprise everybody who knows the value of them.

Call & see the productions of **CHINA & JAPAN** at

ALTHAM'S TEA STORES.

GIVEN WITH A QUARTER POUND OF TEA.

| 1 Camphor-wood Stamp Cabinet | Or 1 Puzzle Box | Or 1 Beautiful Silk Ball |

GIVEN WITH HALF A POUND OF TEA.

1 Pair Blue and White China Vases — Or 1 Pair Blue & White China Spill Pots — Or 1 Pair Celadon Spill Pots — Or 1 Camphor Wood Cabinet

GIVEN WITH ONE POUND OF TEA.

1 Pair of Elaborately Decorated Green & Gold Vases — Or 1 Set of Smokers' Ash Trays — Or 1 Bamboo Bread Tray — Or 1 Pair of Japanese Vases — Or 1 Cabinet

GIVEN WITH ONE AND A HALF POUNDS OF TEA.

1 Very Handsome Silk Hand Screen, with Ivory Faces — Or 1 Japanese Tray

ABM. ALTHAM'S STOCK OF

USEFUL GOODS

Is more varied than ever. The latest additions include the following :—

Given with a Quarter Pound of Tea.—1 Metal Table Spoon—Or 1 Comb Box

Given with Half a Pound of Tea.—1 Garden Fork — Or 1 Garden Trowel — Or 1 Superior Oval Glass Dish

Given with One Pound of Tea.—1 Strong Cullender

☞ See the Velvet Pile Bags, with Cowhide Handles, at 1/3 each.

USE ALTHAM'S JAMS,

MADE FROM SOUND FRUIT AND FINE SUGAR.

A 2 lb. Glass Jar of **BLACK CURRANTS** .... 1s.

A 2 lb. Glass Jar of **DAMSON** .... 10½d.

A 2 lb. Glass Jar of **RASPBERRY** and **GOOSEBERRY** .... 9d.

ABM. ALTHAM, TEA MERCHANT,

Messrs A. Altham issued this flyer in around 1890. Practical gifts to the value of the tea purchased were regularly given away. In September 1904 Nelson Corporation acquired No. 2 Railway Street for town improvement and in October Messrs Altham bought No. 1 Scotland Road for £7,500. The store was relocated under the name of Altham's Stores Ltd. When Abraham Altham died in 1885 there were sixty-four branches, in Lancashire, Yorkshire, Cheshire and Lincolnshire.

Nelson lost one of its well-known characters with the death of George Reader (aged seventy-six) of 14 Bradley View in early November 1901. He was a director of the Marlborough Hotel and a marine store dealer in Ann Street. To get home he walked over a plank bridge that crossed Walverden Stream from the Goit to Haighton's Foundry. He fell into the stream during a fog, suffering fatal injuries. His son, also called George, a director of the Marlborough Hotel, took over the business. Rag and scrap metal merchants George Reader & Co. closed in the 1960s, some years before the demolition of Ann Street.

Opposite above: The Market Hall on Nelson (later Market) Street in 1903. It was opened in June 1889 and was very well patronised. Its appearance was subsequently enhanced by the addition of a clock tower designed by Lord Grimthorpe. Mr H. Tunstill set the clock going on 18 June 1904. Tragically a fire broke out on the bitterly cold evening of 3 March 1932 and although the fire brigade was on the scene in minutes the building could not be saved.

Opposite below: An organ grinder is entertaining a group of children outside what is very likely the drapery shop of Margaret Deluce at 66 Every Street. She also had a stall in the Market Hall (*c.* 1910).

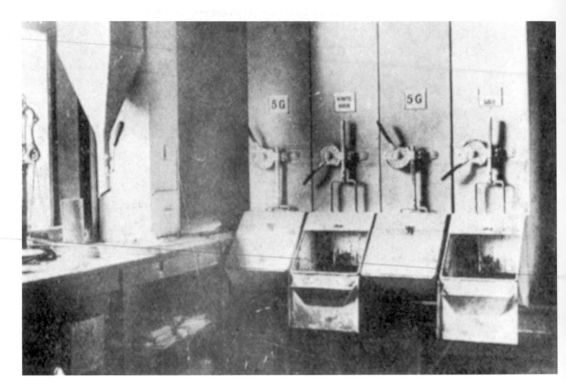

Sam Terry started his window cleaning business on Edgar Street a little before 1908. Three years later Mr Terry dealt in firewood in addition to his window cleaning rounds. At the time of the outbreak of the First World War, the business was at 287 Leeds Road and the firewood side of the business had been put on the back burner!

Opposite above: Lawrence Fryer from Long Preston settled in Nelson in 1863. He had premises on Manchester Road and in around 1880 he founded the iron and tinplate-working firm Lawrence Fryer & Son at 19 Ann Street. Mr Fryer was connected with the Co-operative movement and this invention, a flour shoot, was widely used in Co-operative stores in north-east Lancashire. He died aged sixty-six at his home (1 Mosley Street) in early November 1901 (the same week as George Reader). The firm was still operating in 1945.

Opposite below. James Moorhouse established his grocery business at 62 Scotland Road in around 1887. He won first prizes for his butter and cheese for the fifth time at the Padiham Agriculture Show on 13 August 1904. This photograph is from around 1905 and the decorated cart may have been in the procession that took place in September (not October!) to celebrate the centenary of Admiral Nelson's victory at Trafalgar.

A selection of the musical instruments sold by Robert Robinson at 79 Scotland Road in 1900. The venue was probably the North Street Baths Assembly Rooms (later the Alhambra cinema) situated only yards away from the shop. Note the cinematograph presentation! Mr Robinson, known as 'Bob O'Aggys', was a member of the Nelson Old Brass Band. By 1902 his sons Henry and Taylor were musical instrument dealers at 82 Scotland Road.

Left: William Shackleton, born on 30 May 1842, was a keen cyclist and rode one of the original 'boneshakers' in the 1860s. He was a clockmaker in Haslingden and then had a market stall at Accrington for thirty years. He moved his business to 265 Leeds Road, Nelson in 1906. Mr Shackleton also sold jewellery 'at reasonable prices'. One of his children was Sir David J. Shackleton – 'from the loom to the legislature'.

Below: On the evening of Monday 18 June 1934 one of the worst fires in Nelson's history occurred in the open market. It was probably caused by some fault in the electrical equipment. It took two days' normal supply of water to bring it under control. Walter Lambert's sons had opened the market in October 1926.

Although the left-hand side of the Manchester Road looks somewhat similar today, the buildings on the right-hand side have all been demolished. Going towards the centre on the left, we can see J.H. Brunton (fish merchant), Wallpaper Decorations Ltd, a wool shop and Boyce's ironmongers (previously W. Colebrook, ironmonger). Boyce's still have these premises almost sixty years on. From the right are Dewhirst & Co. (clothiers), Robinson & Co. (china dealers), R. Sharp's bookshop and A. Dyson's picture framers. This photograph was probably taken during the late 1940s.

Opposte above: Messrs F. Newman and Co at 46–50 Scotland Road stocked all the nationally known makes of tyres in the 1930s. Leslie Newman, a pioneer in tyre sales in Nelson, was the owner. The firm held a stock of British Goodrich, made in Lancashire, as well as Dunlop, Firestone and others. Their Firestone vulcanising plant allowed them to handle difficult repair work competently. They were still in business at the end of the war.

Opposite below: A Chamber of Trade ball, held in the Imperial Ballroom (*c.* 1934). Seated left to right are Mr Gurth Cort, house furnisher (president); the mayoress Mrs Marjorie Pearson; the mayor Alderman John Ambrose Helliwell; Mrs Cort; and the secretary Robert Fletcher (standing). Mr Helliwell, a sewing machine agent, is remembered for being greeted by a local band in Victoria Park playing the popular tune 'Mucking About in the Garden'. He did not wish the national anthem to be played!

This eye-catching arrangement in Oddie's shop window at 29 Scotland Road won first prize for the 'Food' section in a shopping pageant and shop window display competition held in Nelson from Saturday 9 June to Saturday 23 June 1951 for the Festival of Britain. The competition was open to all traders in the town and there were three prizes for each category.

Opposite above: Stansfield Ogden came to live in Nelson in 1884 and established a confectionery business at 87 Scotland Road. Mr Ogden later extended the business and occupied premises at 29 and 129 Scotland Road. He also built the Assembly Rooms on Scotland Road. Mr Ogden's son took over the company after his retirement. The business was eventually sold to W.H. Oddie.

Opposite below: This is the Bass family at the bakery of W.H. Oddie on Colbran Street in the 1940s, admiring their handiwork. The bakery was founded in Colne in 1905. Special promotions have taken place this year, to celebrate the centenary, in their nine bakers/confectioners shops in Burnley, Nelson and Colne.

Boothman's Bargain Sale

COMMENCES

FRIDAY, JANUARY 7th, 1927.

Everything Reduced in Price.
Big Reductions in Winter Goods.
A few Special Offers enumerated below.

| Girls' Combinations, 2/6 and 3/6 Usually 7/11 and 8/11. | Ladies' Knickers, 1/4½, 1/9, 1/11½ Usually 1/6 to 2/6. |
| Ladies' All Wool ditto, 3/11 All Qualities Reduced. | Children's Knickers also very Cheap |

CHILDREN'S FLEECY BODICES, 10½d. Each.

Ladies' Cashmere Hose, Black and Colours, 1/10½.	Art Silk Scarves from 11½d.
Usual Prices 2/6 to 3/6.	Ice Wool Scarves 3/11, from 5/11.
Ladies' Silk Hose and Silk Mixture from 3/-	All Soiled Goods Greatly Reduced.

THREE SPECIAL OFFERS IN CORSETS. Reliable Makes.

3/11, Twilfit Make. Size 23 only. Usually 4/11.
4/11, Twilfit Make. Sizes 22, 23, 24. Usually 6/11.
5/11, Twilfit Make. Sizes 21, 22, 23, 24, 25. Usually 7/11.
Also few other Special Lines. Oddments very Cheap.

| Children's Gloves, from 6d. per pair | Ladies' Black and Coloured Hose, from 11½d. per pair. |
| Ladies' Silk Lined, 1/6, was 2/11. | All Reduced. |

Oddments in CAMISOLES, BUST BODICES, &c., very Cheap.

| Christmas Handkerchiefs, &c., at Clearing Prices. | Ladies' and Gent's Umbrellas from 3/11. |
| | All Reduced. Extensive Variety. |

LADIES' WOOL COATS and PULLOVERS, all Cut Down.
SLEEVELESS COATS, 1/11½. WOOL COATS, from 3/9.

Men's Satteen Shirts 4/6, 5/3, 7/3 for the Sale.	Men's Plain and Fancy Cashmere and Silk and Wool Half Hose, 1/10 per pair.
Men's Union Shirts, 5/6, 6/6, 7/3, 8/6, 9/6 Usually 5/11 to 10/6.	Usual Prices, 1/11½ to 3/6.
Flannelette Shirts, 4/9. Few Soiled very Cheap.	Men's Strong Half Hose, 11½d., 1/4½, 1/10

MEN'S CARDIGANS and PULLOVERS, all Reduced.
Cardigans from 3/9. Boys' Pullovers, 3/6, all Sizes.

| Men's Vests and Pants from 1/10 to 8/6. All Reduced. | Boys' Grey and Fawn Hose, Fancy Tops, 1/6 and 1/9 per pair, all Sizes. |
| Few Oddments at Half Price. | Men's Cashmere Half Hose, 1/4½. All Wool. |

GENT'S TIES, 1/- and 1/6. Usually 1/9 to 3/6.
BOYS' KNITTED TIES, from 6½d.

| Few Tapestry Covers to Clear very Cheap. | Few Eiderdowns at a Great Reduction. |

All Cushion Covers, Table Covers, Duchess Sets, Sideboard Covers, &c., at Prices to Clear.
Wool and Cotton Blankets, Sheets, Quilts, Pillow Cases &c. All Reduced.

WATCH OUR WINDOWS AND NOTE THE PRICES AT

Boothman's Bargain Sale.
7 MARKET STREET.

Left: A flyer advertising a 'Bargain Sale' of discounted stock. Frederick Boothman first opened the shop doors at No. 7 Market Street in October 1910 and two further generations of the family gave excellent service to the people of Nelson and the surrounding area. Peter Boothman owned the shop when it closed at the end of January 1988 and was sold.

Below: Boothman's displayed their merchandise on stall No. 6 at a trades exhibition held in the Imperial Ballroom during the week ending 18 May 1935. Several traders had their wares on view. The latest domestic appliances and scientific inventions were demonstrated by working models and lectures. There were home cine shows and 'Zada', a psychic, proved an outstanding attraction. The exhibition's dog mascot Ret 'collected' donations for the Nelson and District Nursing Association.

Peter Attey was the owner of Moffitt's Ladies Outfitters at 39 and 41 Scotland Road when this photograph was taken in the 1940s. The business started in around 1903 as a drapers, silk mercer and funeral director. Mr Attey's father-in-law Mr Sharp had gained employment at the store and eventually became the owner, but the original name 'Moffitt' stayed. In March 1910 Nelson held its first Shopping Carnival. Shop window displays were judged in three different categories. Moffitt Bros gained three first prizes in the 'Things to Wear' category; shields for best-decorated shop premises and shop window and a silver cup.

Alec Holt opened the Nylon Bar at 11 Railway Street in the 1950s and it proved a popular shop with girls (and boys) of all ages! Stockings with decoration applied to show just above the ankle and 'seams' to keep straight were all the rage. Suspender belts were a must of course. The premises were demolished in March 1965. Mr Holt also had a shoe shop in Railway Street.

James Heaton started his business in 1957 from property in Dial Street previously run as a French polishing shop by Fred Dugdale. This was over the Co-op 'Cloggers', behind the Emporium on Leeds Road. Due to increased trade Mr Heaton moved to three-storey premises in Chapel Street and this van is outside in 1958. On the ground floor was the salesroom and the others were used for restoration work and whitewood furniture. In around 1966 Jim Heaton moved his business to the Romany Buildings in Scotland Road and eventually he owned the entire building. His furniture empire had begun.

A Nelson police officer, hearing a crash of glass just after midnight on Saturday 11 March 1956, ran into Leeds Road and discovered the broken window of H.A. Humberstone's jewellers at No. 31a. There was a brick inside the window and watches had been taken. Roger Bancroft, an employee, saw the police investigating the incident and informed Mr Humberstone, who said that this was the third time in six years his shop had been robbed. Goods were stolen on the first occasion but nothing had been missed the second time. After his war service in the Fleet Air Arm Bert Humberstone had taken over the shop from Rennie Duckworth, who was emigrating. (Photograph taken by Brian Duff FRSP).

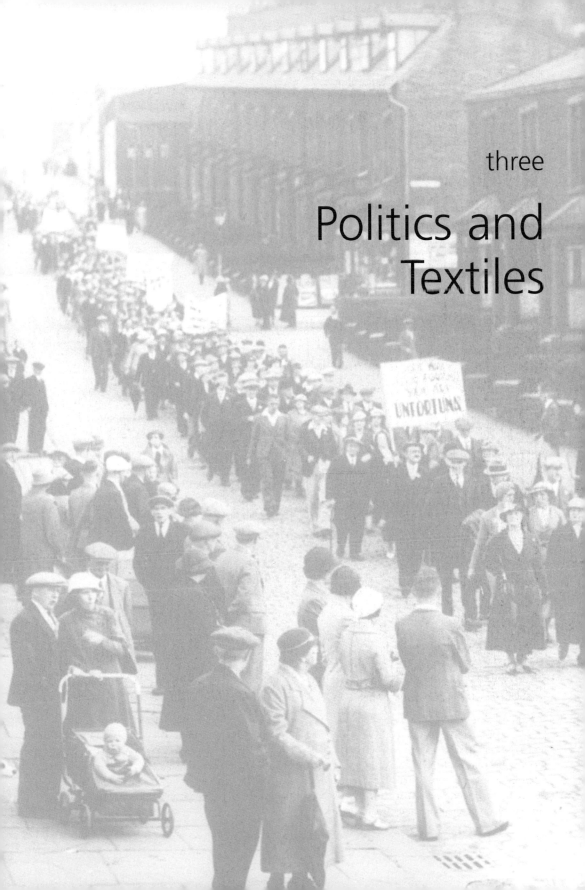

three

Politics and
Textiles

James Keir Hardie in a sparsely furnished room of a working class home in around 1915. Born in Lanarkshire in 1857, he worked from a young age in a coalmine and although his time for education was limited, he read the works of Thomas Carlyle and others. Mr Hardie was the first elected Socialist Member of Parliament and entered the house in 1892 wearing a cloth cap! He came to Nelson on a number of occasions. Speaking at the new Independent Labour Party Hall in Vernon Street on the evening of Sunday 11 April 1908, Mr Hardie considered the building to be the finest of its kind in the Socialist movement.

Philip Snowden was arguably the best-known Socialist after Keir Hardie. He was born in Cowling in 1864 but lived in Nelson for many years and was nominated as a possible Labour candidate for the Clitheroe Division in 1902. In 1909 Mr Snowden, then Labour member for Blackburn, questioned the Home Secretary about Labour's belief that some Suffragists, titled and wealthy ladies, were receiving preferential treatment – that they were being released from prison if found to be suffering any ill health after being examined by a doctor. Mr Snowden was Chancellor of the Exchequer for the term of two Labour governments after the First World War but left the party in 1931.

Left: Councillor William Rickard became the town's first Labour mayor on Thursday 30 August 1906. A native of Cornwall, he worked in a tin mine, but at the age of fifteen William moved with his parents to Nelson and commenced work in the warehouse at Lomeshaye Mills. He became a weaver and vice president of the Weavers Association. Later he became a tea and general dealer. In 1901 Mr Rickard contested the Netherfield ward and won by 97 votes. A pioneer of the Labour movement, Councillor Rickard died aged seventy-seven on Friday 21 October 1938, after a life of service to Nelson.

Right: Samuel Sydney Silverman (1895–1968) was probably Nelson and Colne's most famous parliamentary candidate. He was born in Liverpool, the son of a drapery peddler. Sydney attended senior school and university with the help of scholarships. He was imprisoned as a conscientious objector during the First World War, but by 1927 had qualified as a solicitor and worked for the poor. In the autumn of 1934 he accepted the invitation of the Nelson and Colne Divisional Labour Party to be their Labour candidate in the 1935 General Election.

Left: At the December election of 1911 the Labour Party put forward Alderman Albert Smith, mayor between 1908 and 1910 and secretary of the Nelson Overlookers Society, as candidate. He was successful over his Conservative opponent by a majority of 6,300. In February 1914 a Bill was debated in the House of Commons by which local education authorities would be given the power to raise the school-leaving age and abolish the half-time system. Although in favour of the Bill, Mr Smith voted against it in the name of the textile workers. It was carried at its second reading by 187 votes to 35. In 1919 he was again successful in an election, being returned by a majority of 6,000 in a poll of 22,000 votes. Mr Smith retired in 1920.

Above: This is a meeting of Labour officials, held on 5 October 1964 with Labour Party representative Sydney Silverman. From left to right, seated behind the table: Mrs Silverman, Len Dole, S. Silverman, J. Shepherd. At the last election Mr Silverman's majority, at 1,264, was the lowest of his six successful campaigns in the constituency; the 1,889 people who had voted for Tom Emmott and his Lancastrian Party had influenced the result. The Labour agent Mr Dole had organised a 'Go With Labour' campaign.

Above: The Nelson, Colne and Brierfield cotton industry protest march down Oxford Street, London in mid-1962. They were protesting about the import of cheap textiles flooding the market. At the front of the march from left to right are Sydney Silverman (Nelson and Colne MP), Harold Ingham (Mayor of Nelson), the Mayor of Burnley, Daniel Jones (Burnley MP) and Councillor Davison (of Colne).

Opposite below: Party supporters with David Waddington after his address in the Nelson Conservative Club on Cross Street on Monday evening, 5 October 1964. As Conservative candidate for the Nelson and Colne division, Mr Waddington had arranged a busy schedule and was going to speak at a number of venues during the week. At the previous election in 1959, Conservative candidate John Crabtree's 19,143 votes may have been a personal vote for a popular figure.

Above: From left to right are Goulam Hussain Khan (a mosque official), Douglas Hoyle MP and Len Dole, celebrating the first official May Day (held on 2 May 1978). The lady on the extreme right appears to be holding the ribbon of a maypole. A tableau written and narrated by Mr Dole describing the origins of May Day and the history of the Labour Party and associated movements was well received by an audience of 150.

SCHEDULE III.

School District of _____ THE BURNLEY UNION SCHOOL ATTENDANCE COMMITTEE.

LABOUR CERTIFICATE.

A half-timer out of work for any time must attend School full time.

In the case of any Child commencing as a half-timer before obtaining this Labour Certificate, the Parent becomes liable to immediate prosecution without further notice.

When duly filled up and sign side by the Teacher, this Form must b by one of the Parents to the School Officer for the District or to the C School Attendance Committee at the U 18, Nicholas Street, Burnley, accompa Registrar's Certificate of Birth, or a Declaration of Age.

AGE AND EMPLOYMENT.

PROFICIENCY.

Date of Birth from Registrar's Certificate.

Day _31st_

Month _Dec_

Year _1879_

I certify that *Jane Waugh*

residing at _25 arnold st_,

was, on the _31st_ day of _January_ 18_90_, not

(1) Strike out what follows if the child is qualified for full time employment.

less than 10 years of age, as appears by the registrar's certificate [or the *statutory declaration.*] now produced to me, (2) and has been shown to

the satisfaction of the local authority for this district to be beneficially

and necessarily employed.

(Signed) _John T Hartley_

(1) or other officer.
(2) School Board or School Attendance Committee.

(2) Clerk to the (3) _Attendance Officer_(3)

for the above district.

R k ê (39,608a) 25,000 2—89

I certify that _Jane Waugh_

residing at _25 Arnold St. Nelson_,

has received a certificate from _W. Northrop Esq._,

one of Her Majesty's Inspectors of Schools, that he (or she) has

(4) reached the _3rd_ Standard.

(Signed) _L Hudson_

Principal Teacher of the _Lomeshaye_ School.

or (2) Clerk to the (3)_____

for the above district.

Dated the _4th_ day of _Jany_ 18_90_

Date of In Schedule C

Day _30th_

Month _May_

Year _1889_

(4) "reached" me passed in reading, w ing, and arithm in the standard m tioned, or a hig standard.

Above: This is the work certificate for Jane Waugh, daughter of Elijah Waugh, a monumental mason on Crawford Street. Children who were 'half-timers' worked in a factory in the morning and attended school for a minimum of three hours in the afternoon. This would be reversed the following week, similar to shift work. After working for several hours in the mill these children were often too tired to concentrate on their lessons.

Right: Smith Whitehead, an architect living at Bradley Hall, built Bankfield Mill near his home; it would operate on the room and power system. The first occupants were James Dyson & Sons, who moved 640 looms here from Bradley Shed in January 1896. Dyson ceased manufacturing in July 1903 and Walter Pollard and others moved into the vacant spaces. In 1911 Hindley Bros and Messrs Haighton were joint owners, with 1,200 looms.

Opposite below: These are handloom weavers' cottages, situated at the back of Hibson Road close to Lomeshaye Road in around 1930. Some of the third-storey windows have been bricked-up. In the nineteenth century looms were kept on the top floor in order to maximise the daylight hours, vital in the winter months.

Above left: This is Mather's Vale Street Shed in 1906, in a photograph of Beatrice Short (aged fourteen) and her brother Jack. The photographer was Albert Richardson; Albert and Beatrice were later married. Jack Short was the father of Donald Lewis Short, Barrowford's last town clerk. The card reads 'That wanted in't warehouse. Alreight I'll be up in a minute'.

Above right: A group of weavers is seen leaving Lomeshaye Mill, in Lomeshaye Village, Nelson (*c.* 1905). The Ecroyd family started the mill in 1854 and the majority of the weavers probably lived in the village. Even as early as 1864 the village could boast of having sixteen gas lamps. The houses were lighted by gas and water was supplied to them from a private reservoir. Most importantly there was good sanitation!

Opposite below: A cold winter's day in early January 1912 and these weavers, some probably employed at Parkfield Mill, are standing idly by in Brunswick Street. In the background are the tall houses of Park Drive and to the left are the railings of Walverden Park. A general 'lock-out' throughout Lancashire had occurred because of the refusal of trade union members to work with non-unionists. By Boxing Day 1911 some 18,000 Nelson weavers were affected. The dispute was finally settled on 12 January 1912.

Above: These weavers in Brunswick Street in around 1910 were probably employed at the Clover or Marsden Mills. The houses had only recently been built and the stones were not yet blackened by the smoke from dozens of nearby domestic and mill chimneys. The area to the right became allotments.

THIS BEATS SHUTTLE KISSING.

SHUTTLE, FLIES, OUT PUT, IT OUT, BENCH,

Above: Thomas Pickles of Burnley invented several loom improvements, including a shuttle that did away with the objectionable practice of 'shuttle kissing' – a weaver had to draw the end of the yarn on a pirn through a hole in a shuttle, and any fibres and oily substances present would get sucked into the mouth.

Left: This young weaver in the 'cabin' in around 1905 is asking his tackler to come and sort out a problem. The lad is losing money and wants things put right. The tackler, who appears to lack enthusiasm for his work and is resting on a beam, tells his weaver to put the shuttle on the bench.

This photograph was taken in around 1915 at Netherfield Mill in Netherfield Road. The majority of weaving sheds still had narrow alleys that often proved dangerous; the looms were often spaced too close together. This mill, belonging to C. Stanworth & Son and employing over fifty workpeople, closed in early 1960. Stanworth's had been manufacturing textiles in Nelson since around 1890.

The Knocker Up. 5.30 A. M.
How the Lancashire Mill Worker is roused from his Slumbers.

Before alarm clocks were manufactured, there was always work for the 'knocker-up'. He was paid a small sum to rouse mill workers from their slumbers, using a pole with wires attached to tap on bedroom windows. Roller blinds made from paper are screening these windows. This is a posed photograph from around 1925.

A group of beamers from around 1940, employed at J.J. Duckworth Ltd's Pendle Street Shed, where cotton, silk and rayon cloths were produced. The beamers were employed to 'set up' the beams of warp yarn by feeding the ends through the healds. F. Wilkinson & Co. Ltd were also involved in the manufacture of similar fabrics. Wm Fell & Co. Ltd produced cotton goods. The three firms were all housed 'under one roof' at the same time.

Opposite above: This is a weavers' demonstration walking down Carr Road in 1936 to the football ground, where Sydney Silverman was to give an address supporting a wage demand. Although unemployment in Nelson was still high it had fallen a little. A number of workers had secured employment and there had been a small increase in wages.

Opposite below: Mrs Eileen Barnes (*née* Pollard), a weaver at Lee Bank Mill on Pinder Street, went to see the manager, Stanley, to get permission to dress up and decorate the 'alley' for the Coronation in 1937; 'to have a bit of a do after work', she said. Eileen is dressed as Queen Elizabeth and Nora and Lillian, crouching at the front, are dressed as princesses.

A presentation was made in James Nelson's boardroom in 1951 to employees who had fifty years of service with the firm. In the centre is Bill Higgin, a loomer and twister. Far left is Tommy Eyre, who had worked for the company for sixty years.

Opposite above: These are weavers from the early 1940s outside the mill of Bradley Nelson & Co. Ltd in Hallam Road. The ladies often wore aprons of reject cloth over wrap-round overalls and their clogs often had a leather band nailed to the sole instead of 'irons'. If young mothers lived within walking distance they usually went home at 8.15 a.m., breakfast time, to see their children but had to be back at their looms by 9.00 a.m.

Opposite below: James Nelson's forefathers had been handloom weavers for several generations. In 1842, at eleven years old, James became a weaver at a mill near his home in Winewall, Trawden, earning 1s 6d a week. Later he beame an overlooker and then mill manager. In 1881 the mill he had managed for fourteen years closed down. James' son Amos, now aged twenty-one, had worked in virtually every department of a cotton mill and had managed to save £200. Together, father and son moved to Brook Street, Nelson and rented space for 160 looms.

James Nelson built Gwen Lodge in 1899 on Great Dole Pasture, lot number six of the Marsden Hall estate sale held on Monday 17 August 1885 at 2.00 p.m. The house provided two homes, one for himself and one for Amos (1860-1947). Later they built the cotton enterprise of Valley Mills. This photograph was taken in around 1904, just before a garage was built for a motorcar.

The Duchess of Kent's hour-long visit to Valley Mills on Tuesday 13 October 1953, accompanied by her daughter, sixteen-year-old Princess Alexandra. When the royal Rolls pulled up at the door at 3.53 p.m. several people were waiting to be introduced. On the left here is fifteen-year-old Jean Edgerley, who had two looms in the training section and was the youngest employee at the mill. Jean was presented to the royal visitors and when the duchess asked if the noise troubled her, being rather nervous she replied 'You get used to it love!', at which the duchess laughed.

These newly installed automatic looms in James Nelson's No. 1 Mill were Saurers, made in Switzerland. One thousand were purchased in the early 1960s, followed by narrow Saurer looms for No. 2 Mill. Later 500 wide looms, Versas, were bought for No. 4 Mill (formerly Lustrafil).

The words 'Nelson Lancashire',
engraved on a wheel spoke weighing
nearly a ton and spinning at up to
120rpm, testified to local craftsmen's
skill. This spoke was one of those on
a mammoth 25-ton flywheel, built
in 1953 at the Phoenix Foundry
of William Roberts & Sons Ltd,
engineers and wheelwrights on
Hibson Street. On the right is the
managing director John A.A. Roberts
and at the front on the left is the
chairman, Thomas E. Roberts.

Referred to as 'That Glorious Hour', the visit of Her Majesty Queen Elizabeth II and HRH The Duke
of Edinburgh to Walter Pollard (1923) Ltd's Malvern Mill took place on Thursday 14 April 1955, from
3.35 p.m. to 4.35 p.m. In order to provide a form of 'bird's-eye view' of the processes to be seen, a
preview prospectus was arranged in this room showing photographs of sizing, looming and twisting. On
the floor are beams and healds.

Alan Battrum, the weaving shed manager at Malvern Mill, explains to the Queen the various motions of weaving – shedding, picking, beat-up, take-up and warp stop. Each item is painted in a different colour on this special loom. There is also a dobby to show how small designs are produced on cloth.

Mrs Kathleen Thorpe with Miss Sharples, probably from the training school, in the 1950s. Mrs Thorpe is 'pinning' at Hildrop Manufacturing, the mill that was on Leeds Road. Later it was owned by Fryer & Co. of the Victory V works. It was subsequently purchased by Nelson Corporation and the mill was demolished. The swimming pool, Wavelengths, was built on the site.

The small textile business of Wiltree Textiles ceased trading in June 1968. This was due to the closure of its large neighbour Lee Bank Sheeting Co. Ltd. The expenses incurred maintaining the building and machinery would have been prohibitive, for a small concern. In June 1972 a subsidiary of Silentnight Upholstery and the Brierfield firm Cooper & Derbyshire both moved into the mill. In March 1973 Lee Bank's steam engine was to be pensioned off, despite still being in perfect condition after sixty years of service.

It was announced in February 1971 that Albert Mill on Clayton Street, the second oldest in the town (at that time occupied by Dyson & Schofield), was to close. As the firm wound down nearly seventy workers lost their jobs. The building became a target for vandals and this disastrous fire occurred on 18 September 1972.

The 'leaning tower of Nelson' at Walverden Shed on Brook Street bit the dust on Sunday 24 June 1990. Des Monaghan, site foreman with BPH Contractors of Blacko, tugged it over with a length of wire. Mr Monaghan said that the chimney was very weak and it came down exactly to plan. It was over 100 years old.

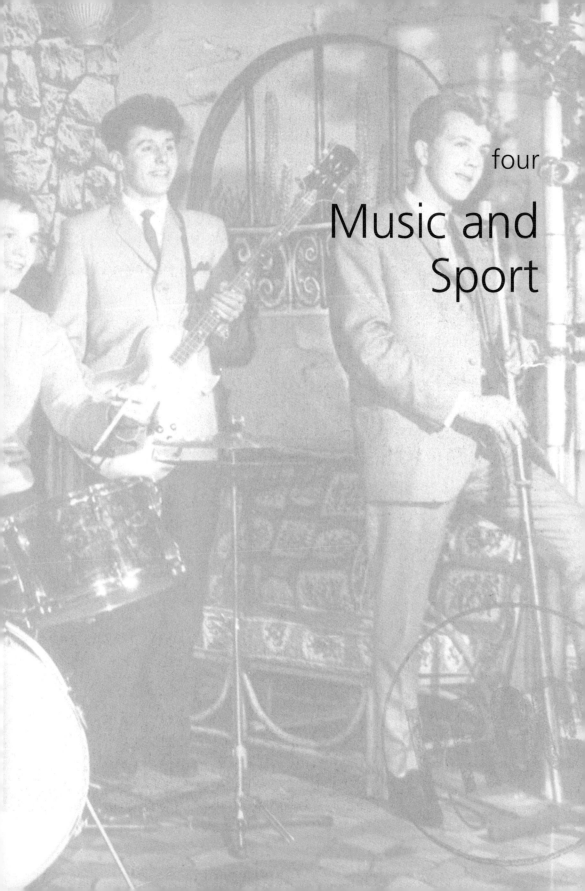

four

Music and
Sport

[Photo by Albert Wilkinson, 10, Percy Street, Nelson]

NELSON CONGREGATIONAL ORCHESTRA, 1908.
(Established 1888).

Morecambe Festival.				Blackpool Festival.			
1st	PRIZE,	1900.	3rd PRIZE, 1905.	1st	PRIZE,	1901.	2nd PRIZE, 1905.
2nd	,,	1901.	1st ,, 1906.	2nd	,,	1902.	2nd ,, 1906.
2nd	,,	1902.	1st ,, 1907.	2nd	,,	1903.	2nd ,, 1907.
1st	,,	1903.	1st ,, 1908.	2nd	,,	1904.	2nd ,, 1908.
1st	,,	1904.					

The Manchester Road Congregational Chapel Orchestra was formed in 1889 and practised under the Revd Mr Richards. Charley Townsley (the son of Richard Townsley, a 'surveyor of the roads' in Little Marsden) helped the orchestra to achieve great success. He was a cousin of town crier Richard Townsley and Nelson's mayor from 1916 to 1918.

George H. Brown CRAM RCM sold musical instruments at 152 Leeds Road (his shop was next to St Philips Street and the church) from around 1910. He was an adjudicator at several music festivals and composed hymn tunes, including a very successful piece called 'Expectation' in March 1924 that sold 5,000 copies. Mr Brown also operated as a shipping and emigration agent from the same premises

Originally members of St Mary's Church Choir, the male quartet formed in around 1883 became the Excelsior Glee Union, under the leadership of Mr G. Walmsley. This photograph shows members of the choir in 1917. In January 1958 the choir, officials and guests left Nelson to go to Manchester, where the Excelsior was to be one of twelve northern choirs making recordings for a BBC choral competition entitled 'Let the People Sing'.

These are the Arion Glee Union members in 1920. The choir was formed in 1890 under the leadership of Mr Thompson. In August 1910 they won two first prizes at the Welsh Eisteddfods. In June 1923 the choir gained a Premier Award for the whole of the country (a gold watch and £100) and in August, as the 'Premier Male Voice Choir in England', they entertained in Lytham and London.

Above: This social gathering for members of the Nelson Glee and Madrigal Society was held in Oddie's Assembly Rooms on Scotland Road in 1947. The mayor is Mr Rushton. On the front row, third from the left is Fred Simpson. On the second row, far right is Miss Ada Myers and far left is the pianist Mrs Horsfall. On the next row back, fourth from the right is Joyce Lilley. On the back row, far left is Robert Walker, with his daughter Doris Walker (a soloist) next to him.

Left: The music shop, run by Mr Blackburn at 100 Manchester Road, in around 1910. It is likely that he had only recently occupied the premises, as the previous owner's name and trade (in carpets, linoleum and bedsteads) appear above the window.

LEONARD DYSON, A.R.M.C.M.,

TENOR.

SCOTLAND ROAD,
NELSON, Lancashire.

For Over 30 years

I have been

Playing the
    Piano

Teaching the
    Piano

and

Selling
    Pianos

THAT IS WHY so many musicians—professional and
amateur—in all parts of the country seek my advice and
experience in the selection of pianos for their personal
use.

THAT IS WHY I was chosen many years ago to represent
makers of the World's Finest Pianos—STEINWAY
AND SONS.

THAT IS WHY I supply the pianos for every great pianist
who has appeared in this district.

THAT IS WHY You can receive Free Expert Professional
Advice on Pianos from Nelson's Leading Piano House

F. BLACKBURN
100 Manchester Road .. Nelson

Telephone Five-One-Three.

Above left: Leonard Dyson AR.MCM, a tenor and
professor of music, was living at 224 Manchester Road
when this photograph was taken in 1919. He also
had premises in Scotland Road, where he gave music
lessons. His daughter Ella gave singing lessons in a
local school.

Above right: Cecil Herbert Bateson was born in 1878
at Park Place on Manchester Road to Joseph and
Mary Ann Bateson. He was an office boy at twelve
years old and by the turn of the century he was
organist at St John's Church, and later at St Paul's
Church. Mr Bateson was associated with many choral
societies and was very respected in the area. A brilliant
musician, he always cheerfully accepted any requests
for his services in support of worthy causes. He was
also a partner in a cotton manufacturing company.
Cecil Bateson died at his home, 50 Carr Road, on 11
May 1945 and the funeral took place at St Paul's. In
June 1946 the decision was taken to perpetuate his
memory by promoting an annual memorial festival.

Left: This advertisement from 1930 shows that Mr
Blackburn had been chosen to represent Steinway &
Sons, probably the most famous pianomakers in Britain.

Above: This is the Salvation Army Band, with Richard Townsley (the town crier) sitting at front left. The drummer is wearing a coarse apron to protect his uniform. The postcard has the postmark 5 October 1911.

Opposite left: Ted Taylor (aged twenty-two) and Hilda Hudson (seventeen) entered the World Amateur Modern Ballroom Dancing Championships in 1925, and after being successful in the preliminary rounds were chosen to represent the northern counties. Sadly family circumstances prevented them from going to Paris for the final rounds. After their marriage they had dance studios and later a lock-up grocery shop in Nelson.

Opposite right: A Festival of Music was held at the Palace Hippodrome on Leeds Road on Sunday 15 December 1929 to provide further funding for the Reedyford Memorial Hospital. The Evmyrion Trio – Marion Shuttleworth (piano), Evelyn Wilcock (violin) and Myra Dixon (cello) played two pieces, the first being Beethoven's *Instrumental Trio in B Flat.* The trio had recently won a first prize at the Blackpool Music Festival.

This production from around 1940 was *The HMS Imperial* and Richard Bateson (centre), a clerk who was later employed with a Nelson firm of solicitors, was the conductor. Mr Bateson was related to the musician Cecil Bateson. Jimmy Sanderson is wearing the naval uniform and at the front on the extreme right is Joan Greenwood.

Left: Herbert Hartley was president of the St John's Operatic Society (founded in 1925) and managing director of The Hartley Cinemas Ltd (which ran the Grand, Palace and Queen's). Many considered him to be the pioneer of local cinematograph entertainment. In September 1930 he married Miss Elizabeth Pickles, daughter of Albert Pickles, a manufacturer.

The Imperial had once been described as the biggest fire risk in Lancashire. The building would have to be evacuated within 90 seconds in order to prevent possible loss of life. This is the aftermath of the spectacular fire that destroyed the Ballroom in March 1976. It was built in 1909 as a roller skating rink and became a dance hall in 1924. In the 1940s and '50s, many 'big' bands appeared. Mr Alec Holt and the other owners made their first star booking, Gene Vincent, in 1963. Probably all the top solo artists and groups of that era played the Imp. Various organisations also had their dances there. The fire wiped out a building that held happy memories for thousands. Flats for the elderly were later built on the site.

Opposite below: The Beatles made the first of their three appearances at the Imperial Ballroom on Saturday 17 May 1965. On the Friday evening some affluent fans were offering £5 for a ticket. BCN Joint Transport had promised two late buses for Barnoldswick and Earby. As The Beatles played and sang 'From Me to You' and other favourites, hysterical girls began to swoon and had to be carried over the stage to avoid the surging crowd. On the left, in the white jacket, is well-known local man Bob Laine.

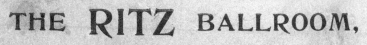

THE RITZ BALLROOM,

Scotland Road, Nelson.   Tel 416.

COMPLIMENTARY TICKET

The Management request the pleasure of your company

on

Sat

....

Your presence will be greatly appreciated.

The grand opening of the Ritz Ballroom in Scotland Road took place on Saturday 30 November 1929, with a matinee and an evening session. Mr and Mrs A.C. Cambage were the owners and Bud Cunningham's Ritzeans provided suitable music for dancing.

Mona and Welbury Petty opened the Romany Ballroom (formerly the Ritz) and only strict tempo dances such as the foxtrot or the waltz were permitted. Thousands of people were introduced to the magic of dancing during the nineteen years the Petty's ran the ballroom. Mona and Welbury vacated the Romany in February 1966 and it became a bingo hall.

Right: Jim and Susan Heaton enjoying an evening of dancing at the Romany Ballroom in around 1952.

Below: The recently formed rhythm group from Nelson, The Dolphins, appeared at the Burnley Mechanics (later the Mecca) with singer Ricky Shaw in 1961. Twelve months later these talented young men were to sign a contract with Doug Sheldon to be his sole music provider if the recording they had made with the well-known pop singer (a song called 'Wendy') proved a success. The group were Bernie Calvert on bass guitar, Bobby Elliott on drums and Tony Hicks on guitar, and they would soon pack up their £800 worth of equipment, give up their local jobs and make haste for London.

Above: Some members of local group The Dolphins were later members of this internationally famous group, The Hollies. 'Carrie-Anne', 'Jennifer Eccles', 'On a Carousel' and 'He Ain't Heavy, He's My Brother' are but a few of their numerous hits. A fortieth anniversary tour was held from February to May 2003 when they toured almost the length and breadth of the country. Bernie Calvert and Terry Sylvester had been members of the group for many years. This photograph, of Tony Hicks, Bobby Elliott, Allan Clarke, Graham Nash and Eric Haydock, was taken in Manchester, *c.* 1980. (Photograph taken by Harry Goodwin)

Above: A new grandstand was opened at Nelson Football Field in August 1923. In that same year the team won the Third Division Championship and moved into the Second Division. They also went on an overseas tour, beating Madrid 4-2! The members of the Nelson team were, from left to right, back row: Bob Lilly, B. Smith (trainer), Edgar Jacques, J. Steel, C. Rigg, J. Bird, E. Braidwood, F. Broadhead, M. McCulloch, R. Hutchinson. Front row: Sid Hoad, ? Black, J. Eddlestone, A. Wolstenholme, Dave Wilson, R. Crawshaw. The team returned to the Third Division in 1925.

Right: Joe Fagan was born in Liverpool on 12 March 1921. Although he was offered the chance to play for Liverpool in October 1938 he decided to join Manchester City. At the age of thirty he left City's Maine Road and became player-manager for Nelson's team of part-timers. Mr Fagan combined this with a job inspecting gas meters in local factories.

Opposite below: A football match between Blackburn and Burnley in 1881 first inspired some Nelson townsfolk to form a team, but it was not until 1889 that the town competed in a senior competition. At the end of 1890 a new stand with accommodation for 450 was being erected, with an enclosed space for some fifty persons. This is a photograph of Second XI team members for the 1893/94 season, by J.L. Hopper of 4 Pendle Street. From left to right, back row: R.H. Berry (trainer), J. Simpson (right full-back), S. Sutcliffe (goalkeeper), J.E. Emmott (captain and left full-back), R. Tomlinson (linesman). Centre row: A. Stott (right half), J. Smith (centre half), M. Speak (left half). Front row: T. Jenkinson (outside right), J. Pate (inside right), J. McDonald (centre forward), B. Wilkinson (inside left), J. Almond (outside left).

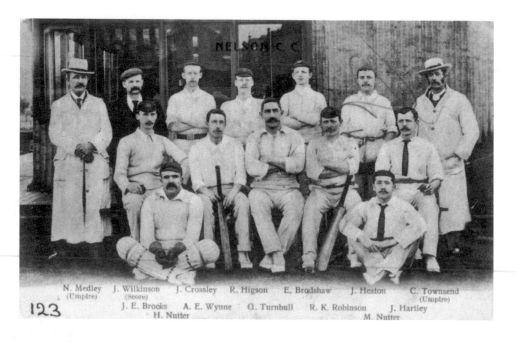

N. Medley   J. Wilkinson   J. Crossley   R. Higson   E. Bradshaw   J. Heaton   C. Townsend
(Umpire)   (Score)   (Umpire)

123   J. E. Brooks   A. E. Wynne   G. Turnbull   R. K. Robinson   J. Hartley
             H. Nutter   M. Nutter

Above: As building in Nelson progressed, the local cricket team were driven from several grounds, until they acquired Seedhill in 1878. In November 1896, Nelson Cricket Club devised an extension scheme. The pavilion and grandstand were moved nearer to the Pendle Street entrance and a terrace was made on the Barrowford side for about 800 spectators. This is the team that won the Lancashire League Championship in 1903.

Left: The local press reported that George Turnbull, Nelson's new cricket professional, had attained a popularity that had not been known since the days of Willis Cuttell. On Saturday 25 April 1903 he took five wickets for 23 runs and followed this up by scoring 74 runs in twenty-eight minutes. In 1906 a presentation was made to him for his outstanding contribution to local sport.

Right: Learie Constantine (later Sir Learie) first came to Nelson in 1929. Although rain spoiled game after game, with Constantine as their professional the Nelson club played terrific cricket whenever they got out of the pavilion and won the Lancashire League Championship. Only one match was lost that season, and then only by 30 runs.

Below: Mary Kenyon is on the second row, second from the left in this group of swimmers at Nelson Baths (*c.* 1929). Mr F. Wilkinson, the baths superintendent at Nelson, taught her to swim. She went to Los Angeles to take part in the Olympics of 1932 when only sixteen years old, but had to undergo an operation for appendicitis and was unable to participate. Tragically Mary died following an accident at work in 1935. A memorial trophy was fashioned for an annual competition in the North Lancashire Ladies 100 Yards Championship. Nelson's greatest female swimmer would be remembered not only locally but also throughout the district where she was loved.

The Spring Bank roller skating hockey team, last holders of the Northern Counties Cup and World Championship winners at the Rink Hockey Tournament in 1913. From left to right: H. Heap (committee), E. Greenwood (back), D. Lund (half-back), John ? (goal), J.H. Greenwood (left wing), E. Healey (right wing), E. Lambert (honorary secretary). Mr Walter Lambert built the roller skating rink in 1909. When he applied for a music licence the magistrates asked about the safety of the building. Mr Lambert replied, amid laughter, 'When I have skaters on it, it is only like flies walking about on a house roof'. In September 1910 he acquired the patent for 'Novel construction of track or tracks for the amusement of roller skaters and the means for guiding and steadying the skater or skaters passing over same'.

Opposite above: The Nelson Golf Club was founded in 1902, with a nine-hole course at Kibble Bank. The club moved to Marsden Heights in March 1917, the clubhouse's official opening taking place on 19 February 1921. This photograph shows the Nelson Golf Club team and officials in 1934, after they received the shield as winners of the East Lancashire Golf Tournament held on the Nelson Golf Club links. Mr J.K. Smith (back row, third from the right) broke the amateur record and equalled the professional's record round. From left to right, back row: W.T. Whittaker (secretary), H. Proctor, -?-, W. Buchanan, -?-, J.K. Smith, H. Shoesmith (professional), -?-. Front row: J. Whittaker (president), H.K. Nelson, J. Holmes (captain).

Members of Holy Saviours Roman Catholic snooker team, winners of the Nelson Sunday School League in 1947/48 and arguably the most successful team in the league's history. From left to right, back row: James (Jimmy) Holden (supporter), Patrick Murphy, Bill Chadwick, Gordon Todd, Jack Hesketh, Dennis O' Hara. Front row: Anthony Cardus, Father Hargreaves, Jack Metcalfe (captain), Father McCarron, Charles Walmsley.

Nelson Town Council decided to build bowling greens on open space close to Thomas Street in October 1910. The bowling team had a very successful year in 1935, winning the 'Triple'. This shows the Thomas Street teams of 1952 with several trophies won during that season. They are photographed in front of the 'old' pavilion. Back row, standing: Harry Foulds (furthest back), Tom Bottomley, Harry Ingham. Extreme right fourth row: Joe Sutcliffe, -?- , Edgar Shuttleworth, Len Hartley, Stan Wadge. Third row: Harry Moore, Tom Brown, Seth Marsden , -?-, Walter Waterworth, Albert Emmott, Alf Law, -?-, -?-, -?-, Ben Titherington, Lloyd Shaw. Second row: Bill Morris, -?-. Front row: Jesse Cooper, -?-, John Stansfield, Fred Taylor, -?- , Tom Shoesmith, Bill Downham, Arnold Bradley, -?-, -?-, Sid Cork, George McKenzie.

The official opening of Thomas Street's new pavilion took place on Saturday 21 April 1956. Councillor R. Wilcock (then mayor and chairman of the Parks Committee) performed the ceremony. This photograph shows the 'A' team, Nelson League Champions in 1964, outside the pavilion. From left to right, back row: W. Whittaker, G. Scowcroft, D. Beesley, L. Shaw, H. Dawes. Middle row: H. Leathley, R. Allen, M. Shaw, G. Mackenzie, R. Carradice. Seated: A. Beesley, C. Bell, A. Preston, A. Edmondson, W. Downham, A. Bradley, G. Briggs.

five

Transport and Haulage

THE LEGION GARAGE

TEL. 1332
NELSON

BRUNSWICK ST.,

An Act of 1770 gave the Canal Company powers to raise £320,000 in shares. Thirty-three miles on the Yorkshire side were completed. Alterations were made to the route to allow the canal to pass by the market towns of Burnley and Blackburn. The canal was finally completed in 1816. The whole length is 129 miles and the highest altitude is at Foulridge, where it passes underground for 1,630 yards by the 'mile tunnel'. This photograph was taken from the towpath near Carr Road in around 1930.

The railway first came to Marsden in 1849 and the halt was given the name Nelson. The first stationmaster was Thomas Carrington. These are the steps that led up to the old platform. After the last passenger train left for Burnley at 11.30 p.m. on Saturday 4 October 1891, nearly 100 men began to remove the old platform. The laying of a new line was completed overnight and at 10 a.m. the next day a ballast train passed over it. At noon, a sixty-ton tank engine was run over the bridge, the most severe test the rolling stock of the Lancashire & Yorkshire Railway Co. could carry out. It proved to be completely satisfactory and a passenger train left Colne at 6.30 p.m. that evening

Above: This is the railway station in around 1903. The stationmaster's house with a booking office on the ground floor is on the right. Several landaus are waiting to transport train passengers to their homes. Left of centre is a horse drawn vehicle from the Lancashire & Yorkshire Bank Ltd at 57-59 Manchester Road. The driver and assistant are probably waiting for the mail train to arrive.

Right: The iron girder footbridge, to go across the railway at Barkerhouse Road, arrived in sections on the morning of Sunday 17 February 1896 and during the day it was placed in position. It was opened to the public a week later.

This is the goods yard in around 1905, looking towards Brierfield. In the background is the crane and the goods warehouse is on the right. Some 200,000 tons of goods were handled annually. On the platform is a wagon heavily laden with baskets and boxes. There are two looms on a cart. A horse stands patiently by.

This is 'Samson' (the goods yard's overhead ten-ton steam crane) in January 1957, shortly before it was demolished. It was built in around 1875 and moved backwards, forwards and sideways, loading and unloading wagons. The coal in the bunker for the crane's boiler only lasted for two or three days and it had to be hauled up in a bucket. In its latter days the crane 'showered' the railway workers beneath with hot water. Driver John Parker and fireman George Dawson were the last men to work on the crane.

CYCLES!
CYCLES!
CYCLES!

Revolution in Prices.

Sole Makers of the Famous **B & S.**

AGENTS FOR—

R. & P.,
(Robinson & Price)
JAMES,
ROYAL
PSYCHO,
(Starley Bros.)
ARIEL,
(Late Dunlop)
AND
STARS,
AND ANY OTHER MAKE.

ACCESSORIES AT LOWEST PRICES.

SPLENDID VALUE ALL THROUGH.

REPAIRS DONE ON THE PREMISES.

Bayne & Son
43,
St. James' Street,
BURNLEY.
Next Door to Tram Office.

Manager:
F. A. MILLARD.

IONERS' TINS is supplied with everything HARDWARE TRADE. ATENT SEAMLESS LOAF TIN.

T. THORP, SILK MERCER & LINEN DRAPER. FRENCH DRESS FABRICS. GLOVER & HOSIER.
11, Manchester Road, BURNLEY.

THE BURNLEY & DISTRICT TRAMWAYS COMPANY, LIMITED.

TIME TABLE
From April 1st, 1898, and until further notice.

SATURDAYS AND MONDAYS.

Burnley to Nelson.	Nelson to Burnley.	Burnley to Padiham.	Padiham to Burnley.

Tuesdays, Wednesdays, Thursdays & Fridays.

Burnley to Nelson.	Nelson to Burnley.	Burnley to Padiham.	Padiham to Burnley.

* Fridays only.   a Workman's Car.
b This Car runs through to Padiham.   Waits for Theatres Tuesdays only.   a Workman's Car.

Average Times the Cars pass Intermediate places:
Depot...... 13 Min. from Burnley. | Tim Bobbin 13 Min. from Burnley.
do. ... 19 „ „ Nelson. | Chanapala 20 „ „ Padiham.
Brierfield.. 23 „ „ Burnley. | do. ... 8 „ „ Padiham.
do. ... 10 „ „ Nelson.

Buy your Tobacco Direct
FROM THE MANUFACTURER.
S. SMITH, 1, Market St.,
Works:—BANKFIELD MILL, BURNLEY.

All the Happy Couples buy their **WEDDING RINGS**
FROM **JOHN H. DICKINSON,**
123, St. James' Street, and 10, Market Street, Burnley.
Every purchaser of a 22ct. GOLD WEDDING RING receives A PAIR OF SUGAR TONGS AND ½ DOZEN TEA SPOONS.
The Largest Stock of Engagement Rings and Keepers in the District.
A PRIVATE ROOM FOR WEDDING AND ENGAGEMENT RINGS.

SATURDAYS ONLY.

SUNDAYS.

Burnley to Nelson.		Nelson to Burnley.		Burnley to Padiham.		Padiham to Burnley.	
a.m.	p.m.	a.m.	p.m.	a.m.	p.m.	a.m.	p.m.

ESTABLISHED 34 YEARS
FOR
EVERYTHING
A
SMOKER
REQUIRES
TRY

J. W. Crook
CARRIER AND FURNITURE REMOVER
3 Large Furniture Vans for hire.
Household Removals, taking all risk
Furniture Warehoused
Looms and Machinery Removed
Estimates given post free.
24, ADLINGTON STREET, BURNLEY
Telephone No. 349

Ralph Mason's TRIPE
IS ALWAYS RELIABLE
SHOPS IN
BURNLEY - - 6
NELSON - - 3
COLNE - - - 2
PADIHAM - - 1
WORKS:
Exmouth St., BURNLEY.

THE BEST AND **CHEAPEST** Place to get **DRESSES** Carpets **SHAWLS**

The first steam trams ran through from Burnley in 1881 and their engines were almost as big as their cars. On the top deck there was one long seat down the middle, with passengers sitting back-to-back. They were often blackened by soot from the chimney, as the tram was open to the elements. For a period horses were used to pull the heavy trams but the horse death toll was high and the company reverted back to using steam. This is a timetable from 1898.

In 1900 Burnley Corporation bought the property of the private company that ran the old steam trams. The old lines were replaced and iron poles erected to carry the overhead electricity wires. Some of Nelson's dignitaries are seen here gathered at the Centre on 15 March 1902 with the first tram. It was a 'Brill Truck with a G.F. Milnes & Co. 64-seat body supplied with minimum of top deck railings'.

Opposite above: A Leyland Park Royal 1933 is turning at the Centre. Mr H. Plowman, the Burnley Town Clerk, made application for licences to operate new services and vary existing ones following the substitution of buses for trams. This application took place on Tuesday 30 April 1935, before the North-Western Traffic Commissions in Liverpool, on behalf of the Burnley, Colne and Nelson Joint Transport Committee. The licences were granted and the changeover took place on 8 May. The routes were certified for double-deckers.

Opposite below: The Crabtree family owned the *Lady Edna* charabanc, seen here in around 1926. It was chocolate brown in colour and named after Edna Crabtree. The Crabtrees were the first people in Nelson to run 'chara' trips.

Left: James Rycroft (1866–1914), known as 'Jimmy Trodge', was the son of Thomas Rycroft, a farmer at Lomeshaye Farm. After James' parents died, Rupert Metcalf, the manager of the Deluxe cinema, took care of James. He regularly gave him free admission to the cinema and an ice cream. A regular haunt of Jimmy's became known as Trodger's Field. Jimmy was a drover and brought the cattle from the farms to Nelson Station before the railway delivered them to Skipton Market. He also moved items, using a long truck with one wheel, for Wesley Clegg. At the time of his death he was living at 51 St Mary's Street.

Below: The business of out porter and furniture remover had been established in the 1880s and Wesley Clegg and his family are seen here standing outside their home at 30 Hibson Road (*c.* 1896). Sadly Mrs Clegg died in 1899. In 1900 the firm carried out over 670 removals using their three furniture vans. Messrs Wesley Clegg worked in other parts of the country as removal contractors for around eighty years.

This is a Hartley Farnell's furniture van near Carr Road in the late 1920s. The Imperial dance hall is in the background. Tom Farnell is on the right.

Farnell's Garage in Carr Road (*c*.1935). From left to right, back row: Jimmy Gribble, Kenneth Freeman, George Wright. Front row: George Pennell, Jimmy Eddington, Frank Holden, Doris Edmondson (*née* Farnell) the company secretary, Walter Smith, Terry Lonsdale, Tommy Watson and Thomas (Tommy) Farnell. Tommy Watson had been wounded in the First World War and the fingers on one of his hands were permanently clenched. To carry out a task he forced his fingers open in order to grip things! As a youth Thomas Farnell ran away to join the Army but was 'dragged back' by a family member.

Left: This photograph was taken in around 1925 when Mrs Jane Farnell (the widow of Hartley Farnell, founder of the company of haulage contractors) visited friends in Normanton, near Wakefield. In the book published to celebrate the golden jubilee of Nelson's incorporation (delayed until 1946 due to the war) Mrs Farnell, of 16 John Street, was stated to be the oldest person in Nelson at ninety-five years of age.

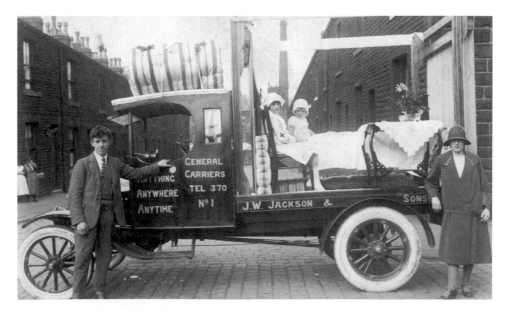

Employees of W. Jackson, road transport contractors. Front row, from left to right: -?-, -?-, -?-, young Kevin Jackson, Crossley Jackson (his father), Ernie Bradshaw, George Parr (father of Ted Parr, conductor of Nelson junior choirs). Back row, far right: Alf Ogden.

Opposite below: This wagon, belonging to J.W. Jackson, was decorated for a procession (possibly the Fire Brigade Demonstration and Hospital Gala, held on 1 June 1927). The young man was probably a driver. Founded in around 1924, the firm was initially involved in cleaning beds and making mattresses (wire ones a speciality) and were known as the Nelson and District Flock Dressing Works (of Norfolk Street). Within a short time they were also haulage contractors.

Above: George Barnes and his nephew Stan Barnes bought the Legion Garage from Harry Hamer on 1 October 1950. There was little trade and they set about building up the business. Around six years later they extended the premises, doubling the size of the covered area. They began to repair and maintain Pickford vans and also the G-Plan wagons, carrying out major work on them. In 1977 George Barnes died and Stan became the sole owner. He sold the garage in 1991.

Left: Stan Barnes at the side of his wagon at Blackpool North Shore on 12 May 1956.

six

Peace and
War

NELSON'S LITTLE LIEUTENANT

Left: Nelson's 'Little Lieutenant', with the help of her mother Mrs Ellen Casey (of 63 Vale Street), raised hundreds of pounds by collecting in the local area. Known as The Lonely Soldiers and Sailors' Fund, the scheme provided very welcome parcels for First World War troops from the surrounding towns. On 16 October 1916 several parcels were sent to soldiers stationed in France, and letters of thanks were later received from Privates R.H. Duerden, H. Hartley, S. Lambert and Gunners J. Hodgson and B. Dean.

Below left: Mrs Casey (of Vale Street) received official news in October 1916 that her husband, Private Casey (aged thirty-eight) of the East Lancashire Regiment 9th Battalion, was missing and may have been killed in action. Mr Casey had been rejected four times before being accepted into the Army in December 1914 and, after training for about nine months, he went to the Front. Charles Casey had died on 13 or 14 September and was entitled to the British War Medal and others. Previously he had been a weaver at Valley Mills.

Below: Several thousand Christmas greetings cards of this design would have been sent to relatives and friends during the First World War.

Left: The first memorial in England to a 'Boy Scout' was unveiled on 18 October 1919, commemorating the 105 Nelson Scouts who were killed in the First World War. The parents of John Abraham Moore were involved in the Scout movement and he was the model for the statue. The sculptor was Job Davies. After being sprayed with paint on two occasions it was removed from Victoria Park, but in October 1998 it was repaired and re-erected in front of the public library on Market Square.

Below: The official date for peace demonstrations in the United Kingdom was 19 July 1919, but due to the holidays they were held on 2 August in Nelson, when a crowd of 20,000 gathered on the cricket field. All the choirs of the town were assembled and local bands led the singing. John Oxenham's 'Long Fought For, Hoped For, Prayed For Peace' was sung to the tune of *Rimington*, composed by Francis Duckworth of Colne.

Above: This 'Peace Lorry', a charabanc from Sandown Motors of Burnley, is about to join the hospital procession in 1919. Mrs Selina Cooper, Nelson's suffragist, is to the right of the banner. Selina Jane Cooper (*née* Coombe) came from Cornwall to Nelson as a young child. The family moved first to Barnoldswick and then to Brierfield. She worked at Tunstill's, where she was introduced to the Independent Labour Movement.

These Lomeshaye School children, photographed on 9 September 1940, had worked very hard collecting salvage for the war effort. Several hundred people in Nelson answered the appeal of the Ministry of Supply. Cardboard boxes, newspapers and similar items that were destroyed could only be replaced by importation from overseas. An article appeared in the local press on 13 September: 'Up Housewives and at 'em'. The collection of waste paper (magazines, unused wallpaper etc.) had reached twelve tons per week in Nelson. Meanwhile the number of townspeople who had offered the iron railings from their garden walls was now in the hundreds.

Opposite below: For 'Nelson's Peace Effort' this march of over 2,000 people took place in Carr Road on 21 June 1936. It was said to be the first of its kind in the country. Sydney Silverman MP is wearing the pale suit and beside him is Nelson's mayor for 1935/36, Alderman Charley Smithson. The banners read 'Friendship not Warships', 'Mobilise for Peace' and 'Nelson for Peace'. A further 150 town councils and local authorities passed similar resolutions in support of Nelson's action.

A replica of Nelson's Column in 1941, with 'Beat the Crisis Campaign' written on its base and a barometer indicating how much money had been lent. In the centre is Salem Chapel, which had been totally demolished by mid-1991.

'Lend to Defend – the Right to be Free' was the headline in the *Nelson Leader* for 'War Weapons Week'. The Mayor of Nelson, Alderman William Bannister, took the salute in front of the Nelson Hotel on Sunday 24 November 1940. Standing from left to right are: town clerk F.W. Roberts; Lieutenant Colonel T. Slingsby; the mayor; –?–; the mayoress; cinema owner Herbert Hartley (chairman of the War Savings Committee); –?–. After leading a procession of local voluntary services, the Lancashire Fusiliers entertained 1,700 people at a meeting at the Palace cinema.

seven

Pubs, Pastilles
and Pop

Left: This is the stained-glass door from the old Lord Nelson Inn. Matthew Pollard and Ann Hindle, a widow, married on 22 November 1790. A thrifty couple, they eventually became the owners of considerable areas of land, including Hibson Meadow at the junction of the new turnpike roads. They quickly realised the financial benefits to be gained by building an inn at the crossroads, and construction was completed in 1805. News reached the township of Admiral Horatio Nelson's victory at Trafalgar on 21 October 1805, and amid great rejoicing the inn was named 'The Lord Nelson Inn'.

Below: A photograph taken in 1952 at the Lord Nelson (which replaced the old Lord Nelson which had been demolished) when the manager Joseph Simpson and his wife were leaving after twelve happy years at the hotel. On the front row from left to right are Sophia Edington, Walter Edington (head barman), Mrs Simpson and Joe Simpson. Mr Simpson had taken over the hotel in 1940 and was the best-dressed landlord in the town. In the postwar years almost fifty staff were employed and upwards of 200 lunches a day were prepared. During election campaigns Mr Silverman and his staff stayed at the hotel, as did the many operatic performers and others who appeared at the Palace Theatre.

In the eighteenth century this was called the Chapel Inn, but the name was subsequently changed to the General Gordon. In 1910 an application was made to carry out extensions to the inn and these were allowed on the condition that the licence for the Farmers' Tavern was not renewed. Mr Eastwood, pictured here with his family, was the licensee when alterations, including stucco painting, were completed in around 1912.

This row of cottages in Hibson Road, The Gravel, was erected at the turn of the nineteenth century. Nos 182-184 had formerly been the Nag's Head beer house. Stone slabs to hold the beer barrels were situated around the walls of the cellar. Until around 1918 No.186 was still used as a slaughterhouse. The whole row was demolished in the 1950s. This photograph was taken in around 1939 when William Bateman, an ice cream dealer, lived at No. 180.

Above: This is a meeting of the Burnley and District Licensed Victuallers Association at Towneley Hall in 1910. Nelson licensees W. Cooper (of the Clayton Arms), J. Barker (Lord Nelson) and J. Riley (Derby Hotel) were present.

Left: This is Edmund Berry with his son Ernest and daughter Beatrice in around 1890. He was publican of the Engineers Arms at the corner of Sagar Street from around 1885 to 1892. There were four living-in employees. Previously he was landlord at the Albert Arms on Leeds Road.

Opposite below: William Dearden was landlord, in the latter part of the eighteenth century, of the Dog and Partridge (Southfield Inn), built on the old coach road from Colne to Hebden Bridge. It became the Shooters Arms. This photograph dates from around 1894 and the lady at the side of the horse and cart may be Jane Hartley, the innkeeper.

Above: Landlord William Cooper had made an application for an Excise Licence in January 1904. This photograph shows the Clayton Arms in around 1905. Mr Cooper, wearing the bowler hat, is standing close to the window of the smoke room. His son Jesse Cooper is standing in the doorway. Note the glass barrel over the doorway.

The Station Hotel was built for Mr William Astley in 1892. Robert Watson (watchmaker and jeweller), Thomas William Trudgill (brushmaker and assurance agent), William Horne and T.M. Smith (both 'dressers') are standing at the corner of the hotel (c. 1905).

Above: This is a Victory V factory train in the Nelson goods yard (*c.* 1945); the posters on the goods vans read 'Victory V'. The goods yard foreman, shunter William Beckwith, is on the steps of the guard's van. These trains ran throughout the Second World War.

Right: The 'monobag' machine, manufactured by Wright's Machinery of Uxbridge, does not appear to have a single scratch on it and was probably brand new. The young lady also appears to be immaculately dressed. This may have been a posed photograph taken between 1968-70 soon after the company took delivery of the machine. A measured amount of sweets were released into the shoot and a bag was drawn from the back of the machine. After the bag was filled it was hermetically sealed. Mint Imperials, Vicory V lozenges etc. were bagged in this way.

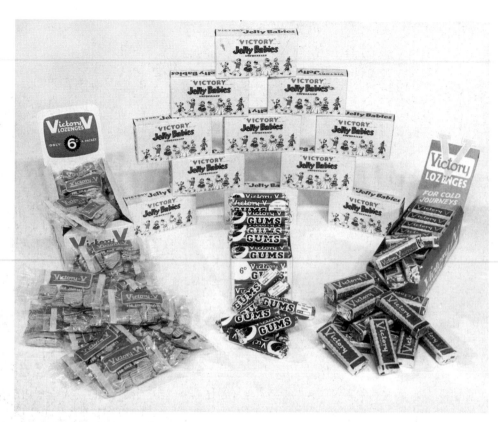

This is driver for Howarth Dyson & Sons of the Borough Mineral Water works on Chapel Street, is photographed in 1918. Deliveries were made in the local area, as far as Colne and Barnoldswick. The company bought their first motorised wagon in 1927. The firm was founded in 1876 in Dial Street and manufactured sarsaparilla, lemonade, ginger ale etc. for 100 years before its closure.

Opposite above: Thomas Fryer learned his trade at the 'Spice Works' at Higherford. He moved with his family to premises next to the Prince of Wales Inn on Leeds Road and had a workforce of four men and one boy. Mr Fryer removed to Chapel Street in around 1898 and the business of Thomas Fryer & Co., manufacturing confectioners and proprietors of the Victory chlorodyne, was formed. In 1960 there were about 500 employees, producing between thirty and forty tons of sweets every week.

Dr Carruthers Smith first produced chlorodyne lozenges at his home in Nelson to relieve sore throats and chesty coughs. His remedy was so succesful that he erected a two-storey building in Chapel Street, *c.* 1814. This was probably the same building that was extended by Thomas fryer so many years later.

Opposite below: Sadly the Victory V works closed in 1988 and this photograph is of the building in the process of demolition. On the right is Walverden Stream, which fed the boiler of the sweet factory before diving under the culvert. Just prior to the closure 200 employees were producing twice as many sweets as 500 employees had in 1960. The Victory Close housing development now occupies the factory site. (Photograph by Dennis Parker ARSP)

These are brand new wagons for Haworth & Son (Nelson) Ltd, mineral water manufacturers on Forest Street. They are on the recreation ground on Carr Road in Nelson in the 1930s. Harry Manning, a driver, is standing second from the right. In around 1900 the partnership of Haworth & Whewell produced a sarsaparilla beer, selling at 9d a gallon!

eight

Fun Days

Thomas 'Peepy' Hargreaves (he only had one eye!) was a remarkable man. He built and owned much of the property in the Bradley district, including 'Kew Gardens', opened in 1886. The admission charge was 2d, which would be thrown into a wheelbarrow. Floral fetes, dog shows and fireworks displays were held and some of the best runners in Lancashire came to compete in races. There were also balloon ascents and parachute descents. Once a man fell on top of a house and broke his leg! The gardens closed in 1890 and the Bradley Room and Power Company Ltd erected a mill. Mr Hargreaves died on 2 April 1896 at 265 Leeds Road, aged fifty-nine.

The De Luxe on Railway Street, Nelson's first purpose-built cinema, opened in 1910. This photograph was taken shortly after the opening. A local pianist was probably employed to provide music before modifications were made for sound equipment. The cinema, which closed in around 1940, was the only one in the area to have a 'direct line' to the fire station.

Above: The flights advertised here were organised by B.R. Nutter, 'the pioneer of flying in the district'. This photograph was taken outside the premises of W. Squire's Motor Supply Stores, at the corner of Manchester Road and Rigby Street, sometime between 1916 and 1922. Later Mr Nutter, a motor engineer and taxi proprietor, kept the Queens Garage on Vine Street.

Right. Mr Barber won first prize for his comical 'get-up' for adults at the Reedyford Hospital Gala (*c.*1930). He added the signs 'I scream' and 'U scream' to the coach-built pram. This harked back to the ditty, 'I scream, you scream, we all scream for ice cream'. The photographer was J.O. Dixon of Leeds Road.

In July 1946, 22,000 holidaymakers from Nelson and Barrowford had their first annual holiday to the seaside or countryside since before the Second World War. Some 15,000 travelled by rail and eighteen 'relief' trains were brought into use. At this time not many people from the local area went to the south coast. Holidaying abroad was for the privileged few. Blackpool, Cleveleys, Morecambe and Southport were far enough away for the majority. The number travelling to these Fylde Coast resorts during Wakes Week surpassed that of any previous year. The stationmaster, Mr A.P. Wilson, said a record had been set up for what was considered long-distance travel.

Opposite above: This is an outing by Bracewell's coach from Wilkinson's Mill in 1935/36, to a pantomime. From left to right, front row: Ethelbert Charles Carter; –?–; George Murray; Norman Baldwin; Joan Baldwin, and behind her is Hilda Baldwin. Behind Mrs Baldwin's right shoulder is Kathleen Little. On the front row to the right is young Joan Murray. Second row, third from the right is Lawrence Murray. Stanley Ratcliffe has his hand resting on Mr Murray's left shoulder. At the back, left of centre in the smart black hat is Ellen Murray. The lady standing on the left in the dark coat with a shawl collar is Annie Bowler. Behind her right shoulder is Elsie Carter. James Greenwood is also featured.

Opposite below: Fairs may have been coming to Nelson for more than a century; Hughes' Boxing Booth visited the town as early as 1897. In 1937 the Town Council refused permission for the sideshow 'Crime Does Not Pay' to appear. It exhibited the ossified, bullet-holed body of the outlaw Jesse James, killed on 3 April 1882. Three generations of the Green family have brought their annual fair to Nelson since 1921. This is the annual fair in 1941.

These are the newly refurbished premises of Altham's Travel Services, formerly Altham's Stores, at No. 3 Scotland Road (c.1969). They acted as agents for companies such as Horizon, Lyons and Blue Cars (who organised continental holidays) and Shearings (for holidays in Great Britain). Holiday camps were very popular destinations.

To celebrate Coronation Day in June 1953, an official day's holiday, this party was held on Garden Street. Mrs M. Mosley, a grocer at 22 Water Street, probably helped with the arrangements. Previously Nelson had celebrated other royal occasions, including when King George V and Queen Mary visited the town in July 1913 and when King George VI and Queen Elizabeth visited in May 1938.

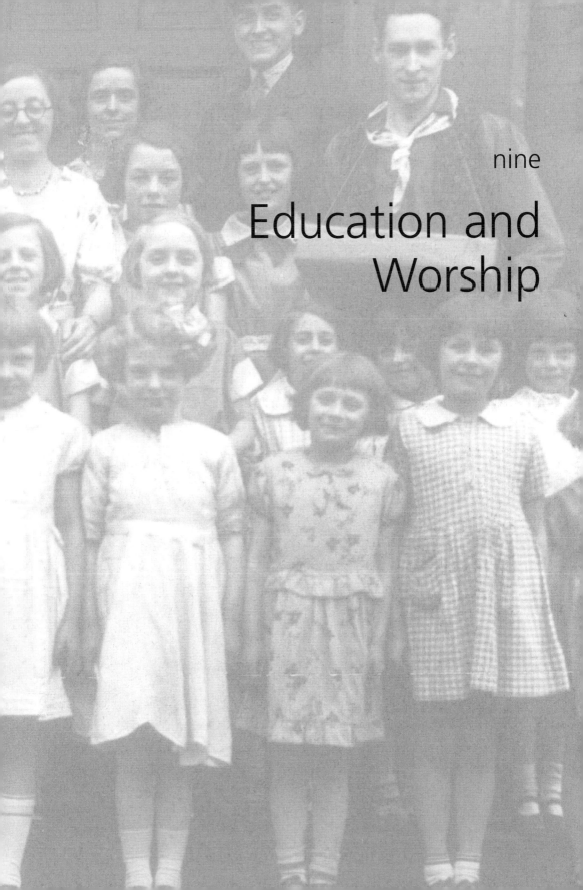

nine

Education and Worship

Leonard Clement was appointed chairman of the Nelson School Board in June 1893. He was born on 9 November 1834 but was soon orphaned. However, through his hard work he was awarded scholarships that helped him to further his education. Mr Clement was the first organising master for the East Lancashire Union of Mechanics' Institutes. He taught in local schools and served on several committees. His death on 12 April 1902 was a great loss to the town. As a token of respect and esteem teachers and hundreds of scholars were among those who lined the route as his cortège made its way to St John's Church.

John Exley was one of the first certificated teachers to work in the town and was appointed to St John's School when it opened in 1849. As headmaster he had a very difficult task trying to meet the standards set by inspectors due to the large number of half-timers at the school. They arrived from work 'labour soiled with heavy eyes and worn faces'. Mr Exley is pictured with a schoolmistress (probably Miss Whitham) and scholars at Leeds Road School. The photograph was taken shortly before Mr Exley's death in 1888.

With
Best Wishes to all my Scholars,
both past and present.

Carr Road Wesleyan School, 1879 to 1899.
Railway Street Wesleyan School, 1899 to 1908.
Bradshaw Street Junior Council School, 1908 to 1916.

Xmas, 1916.   JNO. W. QUINEY.

Left: Wesley Quiney spent a lot of time gathering data regarding old buildings in Higham. M.L. Wilkinson and John E. Calderbank (Higham's historian) had inspired his interest in the history of the area. Mr Quiney, after a lifetime spent in teaching, died on 20 October 1946 aged eighty-eight at 6 Every Street, Nelson, his home for over half a century.

Below: These are the boys in Form 3 at the secondary school, forerunner of the grammar school, in 1907. The school was opened in September 1895 with around sixty-five pupils. John Hilton BA was the chemistry teacher and in 1906 became the principal. Mr Hilton held the position of headmaster until his retirement from the school in 1914. He became a cotton manufacturer at Albert Mills in Barrowford.

The passing of the Education Act 1918 conferred on Local Education Authorities wider powers with respect to the health of school children. The Open Air School on Townhouse Road was opened in 1930 for those with special educational and health needs. Its situation away from the smoky atmosphere of the town provided a better environment for children with respiratory problems. This shows the customary afternoon nap outdoors, in 1931.

The founders of Salem Chapel held their first meetings in a cottage, a 'Dandy' shop at Bradley Lane Head, in around 1851. It can be seen on the right here but was demolished in 1913. The building on the left is Model Lodging House. The notice reads 'Samuel Wright. Building and Property Repairer. 74 Leeds Road'. The foundations for the Salem Chapel were laid at the centre of the village and it was opened in November 1853. It cost £1,000 to build.

The Revd G.A. Fry (Vicar of St John's) and the warders were granted a faculty in September 1896 to enlarge the chancel and to provide vestries and an organ chamber. The old pews would be replaced with new seats. This photograph was taken shortly after the alterations.

Bradley Hall Methodist Mission started in 1893 at Hildrop. This photograph is from around 1905, when a new chapel was built to seat 500 at a cost of £3,500. The chapel stands on the site of the old farmhouse and toll bar. Holy Saviours Roman Catholic Infants School (opened in 1896) and the presbytery (in the background) stand upon the site of the outbuildings of the farmyard. The Catholic school is actually converted from a part of the barn. The Catholic church was built in 1904.

The foundation stone for St Joseph's Roman Catholic Church on Macleod Street was laid at the end of October 1896. The church was built in the Gothic style, with Father Smith overseeing the scheme. This shows the unveiling of a war memorial on 3 April 1919, attended by the mayor Charley Townsley.

The Nelson YMCA was formed in 1899; in 1900 these premises at 118a Leeds Road were converted for the members, opening on 26 January 1901. This building, situated at the corner of Barkerhouse Road, provided accommodation for reading rooms and meetings. The Nelson branch ceased with a final dinner, held on Friday 9 December 1949.

Temple Street Church holding 'Ye Old Village Fair' in 1933. Maypole dancers and others who took part in the opening ceremony are pictured. The choirmaster and his wife, Mr and Mrs Butterworth (on the back row on the left), received the guests and Mrs N. Parker was the opener. The foundation stones for the church were laid at the end of February 1904 and the opening ceremony took place in November.

St Philip's had received a peal of eight bells. Robert Wormwell of Burnley gave four of the bells and three members of the Ridehalgh family of Barrowford and Thomas Fletcher of Nelson offered a bell each. The Nelson Arion Glee Union contributed £20 towards the installation of the bells and the dedication took place on 15 December 1923, when the Nelson Old Prize Band took part and the ringers from Holy Trinity Church in Burnley rang the first peal. St Philip's was the first church in Nelson to have a peal of bells.

Above: St Mary's Church was built in 1878 and the steeple was completed at the beginning of September 1907. On 23 May 1920 a memorial cross was unveiled in the churchyard and in June the Revd J.C. Hill, Rector of Burnley, unveiled a 'Memorial to the Fallen' window.

Left: This cyclist was a third prize winner at a Temperance demonstration held on 29 July 1911. The procession was for the Nelson and District Temperance Society and Band of Hope Union. Almost three thousand people made their way to Farther Lee Farm, where coffee and buns were distributed to the children. Several field sports took place, including tug of war and egg and spoon races, with prizes for each event

The Every Street Independent Methodist Chapel was opened in 1895 and these fruits and flowers created a wonderful display for the Harvest Festival of 1925 or 1926.

The Low Town House Farm Croft party, held to celebrate the end of hay-time. All those in the photograph were members of St John's Church. From left to right, standing: Mrs Mark Hartley (the churchwarden's wife), Mrs Halstead (the farmer's wife, who provided the refreshments). Back Row: Laura Halstead, Alice Hartley (daughter of the St John's caretaker), Susan Halstead, Lena Halstead, Margaret Halstead, Edgar Halstead. Front Row: Nora Halstead (1904-1988, a keen amateur singer, speaker, writer and poet), William Fothergill, William Shackleton, Annie Hartley, Ernest Berry, Lena Berry. The baby is John Halstead.

Other local titles published by Tempus

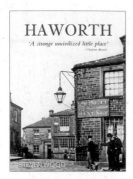

Haworth: 'A strange uncivilized little place'

STEVEN WOOD

The picturesque village of Haworth in West Yorkshire is known worldwide for its association with the Brontë family, who had their home there. This book traces the history of the village and explores some less well-known aspects of the Brontës' connections with Haworth. This book will delight residents and visitors to Haworth with its fresh approach to the history of the village.

0-7524-3508-6

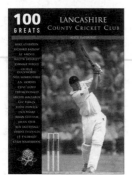

Lancashire County Cricket Club 100 Greats

KEITH HAYHURST

Over 600 players have represented Lancashire CCC since it was formed in 1864. This book celebrates 100 of the best, many of them being leading household names or major figures in the heritage of the sport. From the exceptional amateurs that dominated the team in the early years through the modern heroes such as Atherton and Flintoff, this book includes biographies, statistics and illustrations of all of Lancashire's finest.

0-7524-2405-X

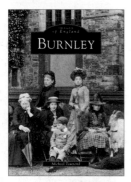

Burnley

MIKE TOWNEND

This excellent collection of photographs illustrates many aspects of life in Burnley from the 1850s to the 1960s. The images were all selected from the archives of Townley Hall Art Gallery and Museum and form an important record of life and times in this important centre of the Lancashire textile industry.

0-7524-1566 2

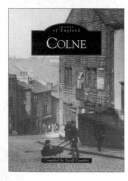

Colne

GEOFF CRAMBIE

This fascinating collection of 200 old photographs illustrates some of the history of this old Lancashire market town over a period of 100 years. The images show streets and buildings, schools and churches, people at work and play and feature some famous personalities from the town's past. The author, Geoff Crambie, is the town's best known historian and the writer of a number of popular books on Colne.

0-7524-2077-1

If you are interested in purchasing other books published by Tempus, or in case you have difficulty finding any Tempus books in your local bookshop, you can also place orders directly through our website

www.tempus-publishing.com